To my cousin
Ernie Lyons

with love,

Lillian Leithead

February 2nd
1999

Limited First Edition

Number 1245
of 200

ISBN 1-878117-11-4

Published by
Lagumo Corp.
Cheyenne, Wyoming

On My Way

Poems
by

Lillian Leithead

ACKNOWLEDGEMENTS

To those friends and relatives too numerous to mention, who have unceasingly tried to convince me that my poems would be of interest to someone other than those included or occasions mentioned therein I say, "Thanks for the motivation."

To my wonderful compassionate friends, John Jolley and his lovely daughter Jennifer, I owe my deepest gratitude for coming to my rescue in accomplishing 'Mission Impossible' by organizing, typing, editing, and engaging in countless details in preparing these poems for press at such a given short notice deadline.

And finally, thanks to my husband, Milo Leithead, who has taken care of the culinary duties and errands pertaining to home keeping while I proofread and attended to other details toward preparing the manuscript.

ABOUT THE AUTHOR

The author's first two years of high school began in 1921 in Primrose, Nebraska at the age of 14. In her junior year she attended school in Spalding, Nebraska. In the year 1924-1925, she returned to her birthplace; Ansley, Nebraska, to finish high school because a Normal Training Course was offered there. Upon completing this course, she could obtain a certificate for teaching in the rural schools of Nebraska.

Near the date of graduation, her class sponsor, Miss Elsie Wynn, requested that a class poem be written by one of the graduating members. The author volunteered to try. This was her introduction to serious poetry writing. After she wrote and submitted the poem to the teacher, she was requested to also write a class song. These lyrics were written to the tune of "In the Gloaming." The Class poem and Class song were included in the program for Senior Class Day.

After graduating from high school, for several years, the author alternated her employment between teaching and a variety of other jobs. For three years she worked as a nurse's aide in the Luthern Hospital in Hot Springs, South Dakota.

While attending Black Hills Teachers' College, she joined the Church of Jesus Christ of Latter-day Saints, 17 July 1928. She was baptized in the icy waters of Spearfish Creek in Spearfish, South Dakota.

Milo Willis Leithead and she were married in the L.D.S. temple in Salt Lake City, Utah, 9 June 1938. In 1943 she worked in the Union Pacific Railroad yards in Laramie, Wyoming. When her husband's work changed to the

Cheyenne, Wyoming area, she quit the Union Pacific and obtained employment in the Modification Center north of Cheyenne. There, the employees installed the latest inventions on the planes flown in from Boeing Aircraft Center and other airplane factories from the west coast of the U.S.

Throughout her life, she has taught at various schools, including several one-room schools in Nebraska, Wyoming and South Dakota. Many years of teaching in elementary grades and rural high schools transpired before her poetry writing surfaced again from her high school days in 1925.

After moving to Worland, Wyoming in 1952, there was a desire for more creative writing to be used in programs and parties in her church and Worland schools. Mrs. Newton White had been a great inspiration to the author as she had written poems for the Worland School functions. After her death, the author tried to emulate her. She enjoyed contributing her original poems in honor of her many heroes and heroines. She continued in this endeavor even after her retirement from teaching.

After her retirement from teaching, on 1 October, 1974, the author and her husband, Milo, became landed immigrants in Alberta, Canada. They continued to be active in Church duties there also. Her poems became a tradition in various functions and programs and were also used in Community World Day of Prayer about 1980 and 1981 in two consecutive years.

Their 160 acre "ranchette" that they purchased 10 miles north of Bluffton, Alberta, became too much of a challenge after 10 years of residence there. They moved back on their acreage northwest of Worland, Wyoming which they had reserved for their final retirement home.

As she looks out across her blue horizons at age 89 years, she views achievements of having earned a BA degree, attending the University of Wyoming, plus 69 credit hours from Eastern Montana College. She has taught 32 years in elementary and rural high schools. The last six years of her teaching career was in Special Education.

Lillian Leithead now resides in the country near Worland, Wyoming with her husband and remains active in Church, other functions and activities. Her husband is still her best friend and confidant.

John Jolley,
Worland, Wyoming
March, 1996

CONTENTS

On My Way

KNOWLEDGE IS POWER

(1925)

"Scientia est Potentia"
Is the motto that we uphold
According to laws of the Latin books
The meaning we now unfold
'Tis the height of the Seniors' ambitions
By the numerous books we devour
To prove to the world and all that is in it
The fact that "Knowledge is Power".
We've finished the "Y" and "Z" puzzles
Of the whole mathematical course
Of the English and History problems
We know the solution and source
We've tramped through hallways of knowledge
On paths of four challenging years
'Til we've conquered the difficult valleys
And wrestled triumphant with fears
We'll stand by the Senior Class colors
Which are the spring green and snow white
With one is marked the beginning
The other, the end of the fight.
The pink rose is the favorite blossom
Whose beauty and fragrance ne'er dies
But strengthens our God-loving virtues
That from every heart doth arise.
Then let us live in this world our great mission
As from sunrise to sunset we roam

That when we receive our last calling
We may joyously anchor safely home.
Now we pray thee dear school mates in leaving
And bidding a fond adieu
Give Ansley High School the best that you have
And the best will return to you.

(This Senior Class poem was written by the author at the age of 18 and read at her graduation program at Ansley, Nebraska in 1925).

ODE TO THE HIGH SCHOOL

(In the Gloaming)

(1925)

When our High School days are over
And we've said our last "good-bye"
We will think of you and cherish
Mem'ries of the days gone by.
When we meet with joy and gladness
Or perhaps some unknown foe
We may banish care and sadness
Thinking of the long ago.

Drifting on these mystic waters
Of life's dark and deep blue sea
Though we've left the High School building
Keep us in your memory.
Kindled hopes are still aspiring
Of the days that are to be
Ever higher goals are tow'ring
From our High School embassy.
We will love you and remember
Days of dear old Ansley High.

(Written for the class song by the author).

3

TEACHING READING WE HOPE

A person who teaches must be well adjusted
No fallen arches nor bank accounts "busted."
A head full of knowledge, "psych tricks" by the
      score
A dignified person with "know how" rapport.
A mild mannered angel with a sweet gentle voice
Who thinks not of money, but the work of his choice.
The children are spirits with which he must mold
Individuality, character, stuff of pure gold.
Our future depends on the upcoming youth
They're pretty good kids if you must know the truth.
But how about adults who should know the facts
Are we doing our best or just wielding the axe,
And letting the chips fall wherever they may
Ignoring the fate of some near future day?
No, we're forging ahead with care and with speed
Doing our best to help all children read.
But what of the hurdles o'er which we must leap
In cognizance of this said balance to keep?
Using Muller's example: review this with me:
And you can deduct what our problems might be.
Imagine some teacher with thirty-four kids
Most of them average; the rest are on skids.
Deciding to give them a test just to see
A standardized test for to tell where they be.
First come the objectives he's met with so far
Then find the I.Q. and to see what is par.

But then he must think of pupil variation
And remember each test score has that set deviation.
Then to add to confusion as well as unrest
Standard errors of measurement exist for each test.
Adding to this are the medians and means
Normal distributions and the spread at extremes.
The intercorrelation of subtests with each other
The personal adjustment of each child with his
        mother.
All other ratings classified "psychological"
Always avoiding the term pedagogical.
Excuse me, a fact overlooked, mercy me!
He's forgotten to check coefficient validity.
And now he detects all subtests are reliable
Allowing of course that statistics are most pliable.
And knows it's not normal at least for his class
For national norms seldom represent mass.
But based on achievement of Australian mechanics
Compared with those working in nuclear dynamics.
Well now if you please sir he's nearly berserk
His native wit leaving, from pure overwork.
But tho' storm clouds gather in fearful derision
The fate of the world yields to people with vision.
He'll stay in the harness, he'll give it up never
And pray that God blesses each righteous endeavor.

SCHOOL TEACHER EXODUS

The Board is my executioner
   I shall not want to teach school anymore
They turneth me out to green pastures
   Where I may sleep
They leadeth me to think I am
   getting too old
That a cat and much napping
   might recondition me.
They desireth to secure young teachers
   for the budget's sake
They sendeth me a "Dear John"
   Yea, tho' I close the school door
Behind me I shall fear no evil
   For I have medicare,
And Social Security will sustain me
   They preparest a teacher retirement
By the efforts of W.E.A.
   They taketh my salary for taxes
And fringes
   My account runneth over - with Master
Charge
   Surely goodness and mercy
shall shower me the rest of my life
   For I shall relax in my rocking chair
And watch T.V. forever.

DESTINY OF LEARNING
(To Wanda George, May 1966)

Life is like an upward journey
To a school upon a hill
Called the "Destiny of Learning"
With a test for every skill.

Achievement challenges within us
Each determines his pursuit;
Evaluating goals and purpose
Often designates our route.

Fate sometimes may seem to thwart us,
Placing obstacles in view
'Til our hearts will nearly fail us
In the work we have to do.

Hardships help to make us stronger
If we take them "on the chin"
We have courage, and no longer
Lack the faith that we can win.

He has given the assurance
Even though we suffer pain
It will be of slight endurance
And the sun will shine again.

There are others you must bless dear
In your humble, gentle way
You must do what you think best dear
As you journey day by day.

So with this in mind dear Wanda
We've not lived to love in vain;
Let our friendly love remind you
In our hearts you still remain.

You have painted us a portrait
Of your character sublime,
And you've colored it with virtue
That will not erase with time.

Write to us and say you're happy
We'll be thankful if you do.
In the "Destiny of Learning"
May God's blessing be on you.

SCHEDULES? ANYONE?
(March 5, 1963)

West Side employs a Principal
Whose name is Robert Moss
And every Tuesday afternoon
Assignments he will toss.

So many teachers he must keep
From mischief's merry making
Or lest in idle moments creep
A resort to belliaiking.

Professional we gals must strive
To be in pace with school
And so precisely on March five
We look upon schedule.

Into those books we surely went
A-searching right and left
Each teacher slaving; duty bent
All pleasures were bereft.

Committees came, committees grew
Our duties shirked? No never;
Into each brain some plan must brew
So we schedule forever.

And now with pride for work well done
For which we hope will please
This little scrap book Bob, you've won
On schedule's A, B, C's.

ROUTINES DISRUPTED

(May 1964)

In '63 the West Side School
Was ready once again
As Robert Richins called the roll
Of teachers whom he'd reign.

Louise and Gladys 'signed to first
Next Helen K. and Pearl in two,
Wanda 'n' Frances placed in third
Just as they're s'posed to do.

There was Jenny Schenk a special one
And Edna Alexander
'Cause Ellen Adams stayed at home
A wearing an "expander."

Bea Stroud and Leithead stayed in fourth
With Gretchen one grade higher
And Hazel in the fifth grade too
Our fledglings to inspire.

We recognize the one in sixth
Rachel, the lady teacher
But Oh! My gracious who is this -
The tall and handsome creature?

His name is Lynn K. Severance
He's sharper than the dickens
With modern math stuffed in his craw
He's outclassed us old chickens.

Well never mind, big hunk of man
You're young but we will betcha
Reports or duties'll get you down
Or panel boards will getcha.

Let's don't stop here, we're not thru yet
The meetings just begun
There're several more that you've not met
Our nurse is Culbertson.

Palette in hand is our Ann Brown
Bertel Budd is in Phys. Ed. we see
John Spratt is here with his baton
And favorite author, Jim Headlee.

Almost important as our books
Or desk, or pen, or chair
Are three most excellent of cooks
Mesdames Johnson, Eckerdt and Mayer.

And there goes Con from room to room
In hall, or where they're dining
Pushing the waxer or the broom
To keep our school rooms shining.

Well time moves on, it will not stop
And Bob is sweatin', swearin'
That he is kept right on the hop
From West to South Side sharin'

All of the stories he has heard
Of one type or another
And keeping track of that big bird
That blesses each grandmother.

When recess bell rings for a break
For toast and drinks or trips of sort
Our Robert says, "Just one breath take
And then prepare your month's report.

It's due today at ten-thirty
You have no time to tarry
You're paid to do this work you know
Don't blame the secretary."

And Shirley says each morning clear
"May I have your attention?
Your tickets you must purchase here
For lunch budget's extension.

My Johnny must balance his books
On this he is a terror
He gives me awful dirty looks
If I make just one error."

By twos and threes kids scamper out
We're glad we have no bother
To keep the charts and money count
It makes our time go farther.

So we can dig into the drawer
And pass those slips out quickly
A half a dozen, maybe more
To children weak or sickly.

It's sponsored by the P.T.A.
It is the humane thing
To stamp the fever germs away
Detected by their throat swabbing.

The kids are back, some work to do
Reluctantly at best
To tackle just a quick review
Preparing for that test.

But flash again, Oh sakes alive!
"I'm sorry now to interfere
The film on "Weather" has arrived
You ordered it last year.

It must be shown at once you know
Three other schools must see
So to the office it must go
At least by eleven-thirty."

So carefully down the hall we step
With children prim or spritely
While Ann hopes no one dares to slip
She says, "Hold paper tightly,

And never mind those passers-by
This hallway we must share you know
And we shall paint both earth and sky
Artistic talent too must grow."

The film is viewed; we've learned a lot
Of sun and storms, of rain or hail
Now if we're lucky, like as not
We'll hear that recess bell.

And after while they troop back in
Their faces hot and red -
"Some study you will now begin"
And they all say, "Drop dead!"

It's time for music for a while
And you acknowledge that
For in the doorway with a smile
Stands jovial Mr. Spratt.

Well tomorrow is another day
We'll not mire in the mud
But fate again must have its way
Phys. Ed. with our Mr. Budd.

By fun and tears those kids do learn,
Life has its roses and its thorns
To face the problems in their turn
And take the "bull right by the horns."

And stay right in there fightin'
It's patience wins the race and so
Learn numbers, readin' and writin'
As they onward, upward go

School is indeed excitin'.
They also live thru season's sneezles
Whooping cough and bleeding nose
Getting mumps and maybe measles
Torn up knees and skinned elbows.
With our modernized contrivances
Flying to the moon, you'd s'pose
Someone'd figure how in science
To prevent a runny nose.

The newest fever has me puzzled
You have noticed it I'm sure
It has hit us here at West Side
And it seems to have no cure.

Lynn refused to sign a contract
To Las Vegas he will go
He was young before this attack
Should I say, "I told you so."

We can see he takes no chances
Slipping down to poverty
While he strives to beat expenses
Soon an old man he will be.

"Grandpa Severance" he'll be never
Storks forbidden from his door
"Class" now but not forever
"Kookie" misers never are.

Edna Alexander's leaving
Going west with her young son
Education they're achieving
In the state of Oregon.

Gretchen's going to Seattle
Grandchildren attract her there
She and Lloyd will both skedaddle
To that place - their love to share.

Pearl Dragoo is going westward
That's the pattern of the group,
Vim and vigor is the password
As she travels 'round the loop.

In the winter we are shaky
When its thirty-eight below
In the spring time we seek Mr. Breakey
What's the trouble - we don't know.

Mr. Haney's here to see us
With a Mr. "What's-His-Name"
He's our Worland Superintendent
And I hide my head in shame.

He's a man of great endurance
Even for a silly rhyme
But he says, "Get fire insurance
Or teach kids in your school time."

Couldn't Robert Richins tell me
Isn't he a good friend still?
Before this tragedy befell me
He should've rung the fire bell.

Well goodbye, but I'm still craving
For your friendship, many thanks
"Leaving fever's" still depraving
Bertel Budd has left our ranks.

Holy Smoke! What next will happen?
Makes a guy feel mighty blue
Jim and Bob don't leave us nappin'
I'll wake up and skip out too.

TRIBUTE TO SHIRLEY AND IRENE

Dear Shirley, and Dear Irene too,
It was great fun just knowing you,
And swapping yarns 'bout this and that
When I stopped by for a brief (?) chat.

But time swept on like a March breeze
E'er we exchanged philosophies.
Each of you bore those special gifts
Of bolstering egos - giving lifts

And making life seem so worthwhile.
It seems for each you had a smile
That warmed my heart, and I must say
That's what it took to make my day.

Smiles are contagious and I vow
They helped to ease each care somehow.
E'en when reports were found defective
You picked up faults like a detective

And tho' I sometimes seemed so shaken
You listened to my belliaikin.
But you gained respite it's no doubt
When I stayed here and you moved out.

And let some unsuspecting soul advance
To take your place and could perchance
Survive the test; but this I knew
No one could take the place of you.

But love expands, yet still remaining
To fill some vacant spot, explaining
How others are esteemed as much
As you, Tho' you my life has touched.

And each his favorite place will fill
And make eternities to thrill
For having had this privilege
Of living here and in this age

When life is filled with hope and song
'Cause both of you happened along.
Accept my thanks for helping me
Seek lofty goals more prudently.

(This poem was written for Shirley Seyfang and Irene Jordan).

TO A FRIEND CONVALESCING
(Doris Lucas)

Dear Doris,

Forgive a woman old and gray
Who failed to come along your way
To wish you joy and wish you well
Like other friends their love to tell.
But don't you think - not for one minute
My prayers for you weren't always in it.
I've wondered what to you I'd give
To let you know I'm glad you live.
This little thought came flitting by
Some flowers soon would wilt and die
So useless then you must declare 'em
You couldn't see 'em, smell nor wear 'em
But this dairy cream is different now
'Twill stick with you and e'en somehow
'Twill do you good and folks can see
How much you really mean to me.

GRATITUDE TO GLADYS

There are some folk who "beat the cars"
How they can keep those early hours
While I am taking "extra winks"
Is when our Gladys always thinks

To plug in coffee pot and make
The beverage for the others' sake
So they can be real calm and cool
As soon as each one reaches school.

And then as if that's not enough
She makes the mugs to hold the stuff
That keeps the brain and soul awake
Enough to help them navigate

Through duty's call another day
And so they calmly go life's way
While cups are hung up neatly so
Each one of us will always know

Which one is which as side by side
They hang with each one's name inscribed
So beautifully, all etched in gold;
A work of art, and this behold

We'd emulate her works in vain
But beg to evermore remain
Her happy co-workers instead
Who have a friend so talented.

May we present at this late date
To express the fact we 'preciate
The kindnesses you will perform;
Each "early bird deserves a worm."

Excuse me please, and mark it well
The last word in that rhyme misspelled
You are the one who deserves the warm
Affection from most everyone.

(Written in tribute to Gladys Graham).

HAPPY DAYS WITH IRMA

"Between the dark and the daylight
When the night is beginning to lower
Comes a time in the day's occupation"
That is known as Our Irma's hour.

The teachers have scurried to meetings
At the beacon of Johnny or Bill
Or possibly gone to their lodgings
To work or relax as they will.

Now Irma thinks, "I can work wonders
To pick up loose ends; I'm alone"
But just as her mind is all settled
She hears a loud ring from the phone.

"Come home Mommy dear we're waiting"
Purrs one soft little voice or another
"We've forgotten instructions you've given,
Won't you hurry home now please, Mother."

"Yes dear, I'll be there in a minute"
And gently hangs up the receiver.
The typewriter clacks like all fury
Irma's fingers are burning like fever.

She's almost all thru with the orders
The clock says it's five fifty-four
She looks as she hears a slight tapping
There's a cute freckled face at the door.

"Hurry Mommy, our daddy is coming
He's just pulling up in the drive"
"Well, honey, I'm ready to go now
I'll be there at five fifty-five."

The door softly closes behind her
Tomorrow will surely be kind
And the day's reminiscing amuses
As it hastily flits thru her mind.

She thinks of the chatter of youngsters
As they come trooping in from the hall
To buy the lunch tickets; they mob her
She tells them "Go back 'til I call."

And teachers will swarm by the dozens
To ask one "little" favor or chide
Then someone has jokes to bring laughter
She resolves to take them in her stride.

Now we pause in our day's occupation
To honor and help to make merry
As we sing "Happy Birthday," and bless you
With many more, sweet secretary."

(Irma Geis was the secretary at West Side School. She lived just across the street from the school.)

TO IRMA - WITH LOVE

Good afternoon Beautiful!
Look what is here
A birthday is coming
For you my dear

Another year gone
But never you fret;
The older you grow
The sweeter you get

Now this is a notion
We think you'll agree
It's time for resolutions
If your new year's to be

The kind you deserve
And this you'll allow
The time we should start
Is right about now.

We depose our resolve
And just it shall be
To consider you first
Instead of just we.

We sorely have robbed you
Without any gun
In taking your time
So your work can't be done
Until the night falls
And day is long gone.

I look out the door
And glance toward school
I'm just looking for
Any lights, as a rule.

And as I suspected
Need I even look twice
No work is neglected
There sits Irma Geis.

Now we're reprimanded
As our conscience comes through
How thoughtless we've been
And especially of you.

Henceforth have happy new years
With birthdays galore
Turn off the school lights
And close the school door.

Here's our latest resolve
We give with this token
We'll try to prove love
With this promise unbroken.

Just send a reminder
When thoughtless we've been
And kick our behinder
If we do it again.

We love ya'
The Gang'sters.

TO LILLIAN

(This poem was written for the author and given to her from the West Side School faculty. She responded with the poem, West Side School, which follows this poem).

We're flocking together,
Like birds of a feather,
To give a big "thank you"
To one of our crew.

Who sends us cards and flowers?
Who writes poetry in the wee morning hours?
I think everyone knows who,
Well, Lillian Leithead, it's you!

That you are a lady with a sense of humor,
Is certainly a fact and not just rumor.
We're awfully glad to have you on our staff,
And at just the right time you cause us to laugh.

So to Lillian our dear friend,
Our sincere thanks do we send,
You have spent much time and some of your money,
As courtesy chairman, you are really a honey!

BELATED HAPPY BIRTHDAY!

WEST SIDE SCHOOL
(1963)

Dear Friends,
The rosebud and the vase you sent
The "Birthday Thoughts" wherein your name
Was autographed with sweet intent
To bring much happiness that came

To such as I who least of all
Deserved your thoughtfulness; my shame
For failure to be worthy of
Your kindnesses, and I recall

As I am brought to realize
That you are each one living proof
Of friendship's test - in loving one
In spite of all the times she's goofed.

Please may this come as no surprise
That I love you! And hope I may
Live long enough so that I can
In deed and work - in truth repay
The debt of love I owe to you my fellowmen.

This can not be; you know the score
I'd have to live for sixty more
But here's step one - I mean it true
With all my heart I do thank you.

DEAR WEST SIDERS

Dear West Siders,

   I thought it wouldn't be too hard
To find that "just right" Thank You card
   That says all that it ought to say
For kindnesses you do each day.

   And though the "bowl" is getting wilty
Each day I feel a lot more guilty
   For my neglect in being kind
In keeping all the ill in mind

   And sending you a "Get Well" wish
And put two posies in a dish
   So you would know we missed you too
And hoping all goes well with you.

   I can't retrace my time ill spent
All I can say, "I will repent."
   I just wish somehow you did know
My love was there, but didn't show.

   So if you'll please forgive the past
I'll mend my ways, I will at last!

      P.S. I'm going to need a lot of help with my mending!

DEAR HELEN

(1968)

Dear Helen:

Life can hold some great surprises
As you've no doubt learned these days
Mixed with joy and sometimes trembling
With humility, for praise.

We don't wish to pose as sadists
Causing you to shed more tears
We just want to give this token
Of our love for you these years

And extol you for achievements
That you've earned by sweat of brow
We just hope your enthusiasm
Will rub off onto us somehow.

Come to think of it though, Helen
Didn't you achieve your best
From examples set by teachers
In your Worland school at "West."

Now that throws us into a quandary
And the answer still we beg
Of the very ancient question:
Which came first — chicken or egg?

Are you great for having known us
Or we, for having known you?
You can see what confusion it's thrown us
In trying to decide who's who.

Nay, jest as we might — you've earned it
The honor you've won isn't ours
You've planted seeds in fertile soil
You've harvested beautiful flowers.

Yet for all there's room for more wisdom
Regardless of how great the soul
And we wish to emulate you, Helen
As you elevate your goal

Of achieving ever higher
There is ne'er a place to stop
'Til the Master Teacher tells you
You have finally reached the top.

May God always bless your efforts
To make better even best
And may He appraise you winner
Is the wish from your friends at "West."

(Helen Kienlen was voted Wyoming Teacher of the Year in 1968).

TO GARY, A WEST SIDE TEACHER

Well, whad-da-ya-know!
  We do declare!
We wouldn't have thought
  That you would dare
To "pop the question"
  Quite so soon.
We really thought you
  Were immune.
But life's got a way of
  Being normal
Some lucky (?) girl must
  Wear that formal.
And collect from you with love
  And kisses
That document that says
  She's Mrs.
We hope your married
  Life is grand
As henceforth you work
  Hand in hand.
This good advice from friends
  Is fair:
Be sure the knot you've tied
  Is square.
In case you quarrel as
  Lovers may

Each cannot pull the
  Other way.
And sever marriage
  'Twill tighter be
And hold you
  'Til Eternity.
Congratulations!
  You affable "cuss"
And love to both
  From all of us.

(Gary became engaged and later disengaged.)

MR. AND MRS. CHARLES BOWERS

We truly hope you will not mind
Or count this an intrusion
Altho' we will admit this time
It might cause some confusion

Your uninvited guests you see
Just simply are a "die-un"
To help you warm your house and be
So happy! We're not "lion".

We've noticed that you're real cool cats
With a house that's neat
So we'll just take off coats and hats
And turn on all the heat.

We hope your home is all complete
With never any stressin'
This gift we give; and we repeat;
We wish you every blessin'!

THE LAND OF T.V. NOOKS

At evening when the sun goes down
We kids are finally homeward bound
We've skated long and played in snow
'Til it is time for Cowboy Shows.

My Daddy thaws the T.V. tray
And Mother goes to P.T.A.
Before I eat I bow my head
And close my eyes while "grace" is said.

And I am back to watch the screen
Before the awful man that's mean
Gets on his horse and rides away
So fast; The Sheriff's on his way.

Bang! Bang! He's shot the Sheriff dead!
The mean, bad man speeds on ahead!
And I am scared but yet I thrill
To see the posse 'round that hill.

They'll get their man - they always do!
But still I like to sit and view
The murder shows, one and another;
And I don't bother Dad and Mother.

Then Baby Sitter yells at me
"Go on to bed - it's ten-thirty."
She breaks into a murder plot
And "bugs me" 'til I'm really hot.

I'll bet that I can be, someday
A burglar that can get away
Why should they always all get shot?
I know that I would not get caught!

WHAT MEETING, BILL?
(Bill Lucas, Principal, West Side School)

So you're going 'bye 'bye
Well, that seems funny
With your eyes both red
And your nose so runny.

Take plenty of hankies
And remember this, honey
Just please blow your nose
And not your money!

Now should you get dizzy
From "car sickness" or "fizz"
Here's tums for the tummy
They should do the "biz"

Bundle up well
And go early to bed
Herewith find the aspirin
For that pain in your head.

Have lots of fun
Be of good cheer
Drive safely back home
No goofing around - dya hear?

(This was read at a West Side School teacher's meeting before Bill Lucas was scheduled to go to an Administrator's Conference in Cheyenne).

DEAR MARVAL
(Marval Harrison)

Dear Marval,

We thought that you might like to know
Our love is with you and to show

That we are wishing every day
Your ills and burdens go away

And times can brighter, gayer be
For you and all your family.

We give this lily, sweet and pure
And this one thing you can be sure

That we are richer, better, far
For such a brave soul that you are

And this our prayer shall always be
That God will bless you constantly.

DEAR MARVAL (# 2)

This is just to let you know
That even tho' the chairman's slow

You're missed and loved by us, your friends
And wonder where endurance ends.

We'd have to search so very far
To find one braver than you are

To keep on going at your pace
And never falter in the race.

AN OPERATION

Dear Friend,

I hope that I may write a verse
So you'll feel better - please not worse!

For if you do I'm sure that I
Will sit me down and cry and cry.

I know just how you feel you see
For once "Doc" did the same to me.

But what gets me is how to find
An answer for an inquiring mind.

I'm sure each youngster'd scoff'n frown
If I'd just say you can't sit down.

And so I just leave them without
An inkling of what it's about.

But anyway we all agree
That we all crave your company.

MY PRECIOUS DISCOVERY!

A world of deep mystery shrouded her
   there
The dark eyed young lady with lovely
   brown hair
And tho' she lived slightly over the
   street
Our paths never knew wherein channels
   to meet.

Her husband seemed shy, reserved,
   but still
I learned in a round about way he
   was "Bill"
The surname I couldn't be sure to
   relate
Was it Ferguson - Fergerson? I couldn't
   keep straight.

And equally puzzled I was, of their
   kin
For which was Diane and which girl
   was Lynn?
The youngest, a boy, I'd bet was the
   boss
Occasionally I heard him referred to
   as Ross.

It was just a short distance; was this
  family
I didn't know them and they didn't
  know me.
And I guess if "fate" hadn't altered
  things as they lay
The Leitheads and Fergersons would
  have kept living that way.

Well, Irma left West Side and I
  in despair
Said no one could quite fill the vacancy
  there.
But startled was I when I heard by "grape
  vine"
The North Side lament was equal
  to mine.

For they loved their lady and unwilling
  to share
Their affable friend with the dusky brown
  hair.
The West Side had gained and the North
  lost no doubt
Before I had learned what they were
  grieving about.

But now it is plain as the nose on your
    face
That you can't find a person you can
    look everyplace
Whom you can love more; she makes your
    heart sing
And makes your load light like a bird on
    the wing.

And talk about talents! She has them
    galore!
You detect it the minute you step in her
    door.
Artistic is spelled with a capital
    "A"
In her painting, in hand crafts; they're
    clever and gay.
In sewing and cooking, in housekeeping
    and charm
A wife, a mother, a friend who
    is warm
In affection and love, and a worker
    like steel
To accomplish so much, how can she be
    real?

I am sure it would take an
　　eternity
To make me become as skillful
　　as she.
Now Marian, this poem has been long
　　overdue
For I never could think of one worthy
　　of you.

Words can't describe your value
　　to me
And the love that I have, but now do
　　you see
I have lost precious years - (and this
　　lesson is hard)
When I failed to discover who's beyond
　　my back yard.

GOOD OLD DAYS (?)

"Good Old Days" weren't any joker
After trudging thru the snow
   What we'd give for a good stoker
So we wouldn't have to go
   Thru the ordeal of long waiting
For a little warmth to come
   Fanning sparks is aggravating
When one's hands and feet are numb.

"Fresh air is so beneficial"
Said some well meaning galoot
   And you'd make the words official
If you've ever inhaled soot
   From a fiendish stove's explosion
Belching smoke into the air
   And you feel the ashes settle
On your clothes and in your hair.

You can wash your blackened nostrils
And once more you might look nice
   After you have thawed the bucket
That is now so bulged with ice.
   Courage now, the fire is burning
And the stove glows with a heat
   That proves you're among the living;
Pains shoot thru your hands and feet.

As you thaw first back then forward
Blessings now seem more secure
   Room and mind now both are clearing
As you close windows and door.
   Blessings yes, but you are dreaming
Of a time, oh so remote
   That someday - with careful scheming
You won't have to wear your coat

   'Til it's ten o'clock or after
Children's teeth are chattering still
   They're too cold to think of laughter
And their minds you can not fill.
   Even tho' the stove is dancing
With a belly full of coal
   Winter's blast has penetrated
Flesh and bones and even soul.

   Schools were burning or decaying
As old schools are prone to do
   God heard teachers in their praying
Said, "I'm sending help to you."
   I've created one you'll welcome
In your hour of deep despair
   He is like the good Samaritan
Who will heed your every care.
   So we had the good man Salzman
Who was extra good 'tis true

And it seemed that there was nothing
That this one man couldn't do.
   Footprints in the halls of study
Don't erase like sands of time
   Nor do prints on walls and windows
Left by little hands with grime.

   Mr. Salzman please, we need you
Some one hurried, but too late
   We want fresh air, mop, and bucket
Johnny's sick and couldn't wait
   Sink's too far or even basket
When one must regurgitate.
   School health nurse is called as fast as
We can all communicate.

   Mr. Salzman was a wonder
Taking care of so much bother
   Cleaning here and minding always
Helping someone like a father.
   If those games of ball or tether
Ended with some enmity
   Snarls and problems somehow shriveled
Thru this kind authority.

   He could settle many riots
Kindled by some little spat
   Troubles soon were all abated
When this man "went out to bat."

"Kill the Umpire" was ne'er spoken
Cause the game was always fair
   And there was no room for cheating;
Who would try or even dare?

   But it seems we have an "Uncle"
Who says "John, its time to quit."
   They will wear you to a frazzle;
You'll have time now just to sit
   And remember all the old days
And the things you used to do
   Or perhaps create a hobby
That will make good use of you.

   Your co-workers wish to thank you.
For those many things you've done
   And we'll bet you'll fool old "Uncle"
In the years that are to come.
   You'll not sit and twiddle fingers
Or decay in idleness
   You'll be busy as the dickens
Or we all have missed our guess.

   Farewell, and thanks for better ways
As you improved those "GOOD OLD DAYS."

SENIOR CITIZENS' BALL

'Twas an elegant party at Nielsen's
   (on the hill)
In honor of Clifford, Jenny, Sally and
   Lil.
Kirk met us at the door with a sly little
   grin
And said, "Howdy folks just come right on
   in".
We eased thru the hall and on down the
   stairs
Where guests were drinking punch, and
   'most unaware
I had what you might call a double
   attack
A "corsage" on my front and a label
   pinned back
Upon which was written a word—as a rule
   Reminded of duties pertaining to school
This one little word they said "you
   must guess"
And all queries made were given a "no"
   or a "yes."
But some who were hungry and kind
   hearted too
Helped this writer along with many a
   clue.

So we were allowed to advance to the
  food
And putting it mildly it was "sure"
  mighty good.
And just as the banquet was barely
  consumed
The tables were suddenly whisked out of
  the room.
And here came some gals with those gleams
  in their eyes
And you knew you were in for another
  surprise.
It seems that Virginia, that sly little
  fox
Had taped school room noises and many
  "shop talks"
Just to help us remember the routine
  and rules
And pity the poor souls who remain
  in the schools.

(Eat your hearts out, you youngsters
  We're free as the breeze
And scurrying like church mice with
  no crackers or cheese.
'Cause we can go fishin' and travelin'
  and such
Oh sure we will miss you but we hope
  not too much).

But back to the party—I'm side-tracked
its true
Over silly remarks and toasts that
began with
C.O.H.L.D. "Come on help Lillian damn
it!"
And a contest with cups of ten jelly
beans
To toss at an open mouth 'mid laughters
and screams
We found out the winners when contests
were done
Were the accurate Marval and Ray
Harrison.
But fun for the evening as all things
must end,
And finally "good nights" came from
each smiling friend.
Dear Helen and Virginia, my thanks as
your guest
And with God's choicest favors may you
always be blessed.

A WHO'S WHO IN WORLAND

Who is this man Alex
Of whom we should write
And wish Happy Birthday!
On this Wednesday night?

"Tell us something about him."
We asked of someone,
"Why is he important
Or what has he done?"

"Well, haven't you noticed
Or must we tell you?
In spite of the weather
The mail has come through

And all of the orders
Whether great: whether small
In the little school truck
He will cheerfully haul.

And in through the door
Glides huge cargo and packet
He's here and he's gone
Without any racket.

He has a sly smile
And a gleam in his eye
He's a "minds his own business"
Sort of a guy.

At delivering gossip
He is no go-getter
His lips are sealed tight
As the flap on a letter.

He's not anti-social
He has many friends
His temper he governs
He needs make no amends.

His duty he renders
Without grumbles or frets
All favors he tenders
Not one he forgets.

He works like a timer
He's so systematic
You can check with your watches
He's never erratic.

No lost golden moments
On his record is found
In his four years of service
Were no strikes nor "sit downs."

Now how can it be
That so long we've neglected
To sing out our praises
To a man so respected?

It just goes to prove
As we drift like a breeze
"We can't see the forest
Because of the trees."

Great men are around us
They're not all in a book,
We've found it rewarding
In just this brief look.

So Alex we thank you
We deem you first rate.
And proudly acclaim you
Our "Alexander the Great."

And as you continue
Your labor with care
We want you to know
That we now are aware

Of the valuable man
To whom we're in debt
For the goodness you share
And example you set.

We know you now Alex
And tribute extend
May you have happy birthdays
Again and again!

(Written for Alex Schaff on his birthday).

TO MARGIE - MY TEACHER'S AIDE
(Margie Fisher)

It's Christmas! And time to express
Our thanks to our God
For his Son which he blessed
And placed upon earth so such sinners as we
Can return to His presence for eternity.
He loved us and so He has shown us the way
To live in this world as it is e'en today.
My load here is easy - or lighter by far
You're an angel of mercy! Yes that's what you are!
And I'd love to tell you
Along with this gift
That I love you and thank you
For giving a lift
And making life brighter and much gayer too.
God bless you this Christmas
And all next year too!

OVER THE HILL! A NEW ONE STILL!

Over the hill to retirement
"I am wending my weary way"
Because I am 'most five years and sixty
I was 'ax-terminated' today.

That's one way to look at a chapter
When nearing the end of a book
But was it an interesting story?
I'll give it another quick look.

Yes, those wonderful mem'ries I treasure
More precious than silver or gold
Some sorrows; but joys without measure
So why should I help getting old?

Now the book of "School Teaching" is over
And in spite of some aches it was fun
But life has its times to be sober
So what if some tears start to run?

The first breath I took on this planet
I cried, 'though I didn't know why
And who knows how many more teardrops
Are required in this "growing up" try?

But as surely as sunshine dries raindrops
And shadows are gently o'ercome
The teardrops are simply refreshers
For a bright and new future to come.

And what if new steps are bewildering
And I falter e'er the race is yet won?
My "new life" will still be exciting
With a purpose; and prayerfully done.

So "Amen" dear school days behind me
I shall welcome adventure to come,
Whatever my efforts in future shall be
May it ever mark progress well done.

SIGMA'S STAR

No one need to search outer space
To discover an unusual star;
Tho' out of this world with talents to place
Each little comet propelled to her door.

Pat Wilcox receives little charges with charm,
Who descend from their orbit in tears;
Reluctant to leave secure parental arms
That also reveal heart aches and fears.

But by unfeigned affection and concern reassured
All the patrons who have apprehensions
That this loving teacher in her overtures
Is genuine with lofty intentions.

Tears turn to smiles; Pat's recompense
While introducing to her magic sphere
Those little angels for whom she'll dispense
Unbelievable fun in learning this year.

Gently, so gently, but consistently firm;
Her designs for little minds molded,
Old patterns displaced as they persistently squirm
In resisting the challenge of progress unfolded.

So much could be said for Pat's patience untold
In her innovative plans for each day;
Directing paths of each precious soul
Who in wisdom will follow her way.

Thirty-one years Pat has successfully taught
In the grades from pre-kindergarten to third;
We honor this lady as everyone ought
As she continues to teach and increase standards.

With teachers like Pat it is easy to see
Why Wyoming's schools are first rate;
She deserves highest praise for such quality
For many long hours, working early and late.

Teacher of the year! What year do they mean?
Ask any little laddie or lass;
She's teacher of every year and everyone's dream
To have the good fortune to be in her class.

These praises of Pat are long overdue
And this message these lines are intending
To express love and appreciation for excellent work
          done;
Sigma's prayers and praise for her never ending.

A CHRISTMAS "STORY"

We shot up the alleys and cut across
  streets
In an effort to purchase some Personnel
  treats.
We jumped to a huddle, then onward we
  sped
Each clever suggestion got a nod of
  each head.
The shopping went fast as a sharp
  western breeze
We were sure that no gifts were much
  nicer than these.
We were shopping like blazes, as I told you
  until
We came to the man on our list that
  was Bill.
We ruled out the usual cuff links and
  neck tie
Shirts, belt, or two socks did not
  get the "Aye."
Well, "gals" we must hurry
  our time has worn thin
We're out of ideas and the meter
  needs "tin".
"Let's go to the car and confer"
  said Louise,

We were sure that we could find a
    notion to please.
Then Hazel came up with a gleam in
    her eyes
"I've got it," she said, "We will
    all compromise;
We'll give him a picture I'm sure that
    will win."
"Of whom?" I was gasping, - she said
    it again.
"A picture of one of ten most
    wanted men."
Now open your gift to see
    what's inside
We hope you will like it—excuse us—
    we tried.
Now joking is ended:
    We're meaning this true
It really was fun going shopping
    for you.

MERRY CHRISTMAS AND A HAPPY NEW
    YEAR!

'TWAS SOMETIME BEFORE CHRISTMAS

'Twas sometime before Christmas
You can laugh if you choose
But Kirk and Virginia awoke
From a snooze.

And checked on the children
Tucked in beds with such care
Then looked at the horses
Breathing frost laden air.

They looked at each other
And tried to surmise
What the heck that it was
Drove the sleep from their eyes.

I know what it is
Exclaimed Virginia in glee
The spirit of Christmas
Has just captured me!

"You've got to be kidding!"
Said Kirk shaking his head,
"The Thanksgiving turkey
Has not long been dead."

"Well granted you're right,"
Said his wife in elation
"But just twenty-one days
'Til it's Christmas vacation."

"So let's have a party
Now we have this big house
Invite all the staff members
Bosses and spouse."

"Hold on just a minute,"
admonished her Kirk
"I don't mind the fun, but
Who'll do the work?"

"I was just going to tell you,"
Said Virginia again
"We'll solicit the help of
Several good men."

"Oh ho!" said tall Kirk
With nary a grumble.
"I think I am almost
Beginning to tumble."

"The plot has been laid
And it now seems to me
You've been premeditating
And just who are we?"

"Well Jennie, and Hazel
And Marvel and I
Were talking of taking
A date on the sly,

From a calendar Bill says
Belongs to the school
We'd hog-tie it early and
Play it real cool."

We'd rope in a figure
Before anyone
Could drop a loop
And lasso all the fun.

This party's tradition
We were wont to remember
No hunting nor fishing
The fourteenth of December."

"But plans have to be altered"
Said Bill, "it is seen,
Junior High has it haltered.
So we captured fifteen."

"Well I see it's all settled,"
Said Kirk with a grin,
"and I reckon the heavy work's
Up to us men.

So haul out your orders and
Dust the Welcome mat,
We'll show those West Siders
Where the action is at."

So into the plans
Those hostesses flew
With Kirk, Clifford, and John
And Ray Harrison too.

Until they made everything
Festive and bright
For their guests to enjoy
On this cool wintry night.

There are cocktails, and hors d'oeuvres
So somebody said
And turkey and vegetables
And rolls for the bread.

And salads galore
Of about every hue
Then pie for dessert, when you
Should think you're through.

Now who could deny as you're
Stuffed to the gills
The spirit of Christmas glows
Warm in these hills.

So let it catch up with you
Here's a good time to start
Being merry this Christmas
With a song in your heart.

CHRISTMAS CARD
(Bluffton, Alberta, Dec. 1976)

You deserve a prettier card
Easily found in most any station
But let this express our regard
For you in this humble creation.

We think the Saviour's intent
Was not to exceed fancy fashion
But rather our talents are spent
In serving with loving compassion.

May the Heavenly Father bless you we pray
With good health in the coming New Year
May happiness be yours as you prosper each day
In the lofty ambitions you rear.

SANTA'S CONVERSION

Missionaries are sent to every land
To search out souls willing to stand
And be counted with Saints of Latter-days
Learning the true Gospel and changing ways.

One time when proselyting was slow
Elders Telford and Barnes had nowhere to go.
Knowing full well they should seek out each soul
They decided to fly straight to the North Pole.

They hadn't seen Santa since they were quite small
So why not just go and pay him a call.
They were greeted so slightly by Santa's wee elves;
The Elders stood staring in spite of themselves.

For there in the midst of toys to his ears
Was Santa sweating and toiling and nearly in tears
So moved with compassion these Elders did say:
"Dear Brother, let us help you, we'll work without
    pay."

So they summoned the elves who had been out on
    strike
And taught them the Gospel that very night.
Tears streamed down their faces as they sat on toad
    stools
As they desired to repent and obey golden rules.

Old Santa was listening and converted was he
And became just as saintly as Santas could be.
They all were baptized by the Elders flown in
And straightway confirmed and forgiven of sin.

They even taught Rudolph some wisdom we hear;
Repentance was done by this red-nosed reindeer.
So now when descending to housetops at nights
You'll see him just blinking the great Northern
      Lights.

Yes, the Elders worked hard in their mission no
      doubt,
In teaching The North what Mormonism's about.
And Santa in gratitude bowed on his knees
To thank the good Lord for sending these Yankees.

To share the Good Word at this time of the year
Bringing joy to the land of the tiny reindeer.
He sought to consult these young Elders who knew
Just how all the members of Rimbey Branch do.

He noticed the lists of the Saints were not long
And wanted to know if something was wrong.
The Elders discreet and meek as a mouse,
Replied, "No Brother Nicholas, they want a Church
      House."

"Ho! Ho!" cried St. Nicholas looking them
        through,
"I've never heard anything better, have you?"
    "So here is the thing I'm suggesting this year
And kindly announce this to Brother Langmuir."

    "Save every penny; tell the good girls and boys
I'll help in their building by bringing less toys
    Though dolls have been ordered, I suppose you
        have heard
By the Taylors and Stuckarts from the 'long legged
    bird'."

    "Each new little member will help your Branch
        grow
And add to the ones you will friendship, you know
    I'm noting the rest of the members you've got
The Rompains and Wettsteins, who help you a lot."

    "The Waltons, Rennakers, Langmuirs and Cahoons
Who teach you and preach you and sing heavenly
        tunes
    The Leitheads, the Hoppers, the Rodes, Purnells,
Jacksons, Hunts, Hersches, and Tanner as well."

There are prospects of others your building to fill
If all will keep working and never sit still.
    Reminiscing the past when the year's work is done
You've all worked together and managed some fun.

The brethren grew "taters" and sisters sewed quilts
In their efforts to fatten the substitute tills.
The children did well as they helped in the field
And also brought pennies from their labor's yield.

"You do need a Meeting House," said St. Nick with
   a grin
"And please build a chimney so I can get in.
   I want to hear music and songs of the star
That shone over Bethlehem's stable so far."

"Then after you've worshipped Him so reverently
Sometimes at a party sing some songs about me.
   Let me hear the accordion, piano, guitars
And yodelers, song birds, actors and stars."

"Let plumbers, carpenters, teachers of school,
Artists, ranchers, barber and ham operator so cool.
   Cowboys, welders, bus driver, truck drivers and
      more
Sing and play carols as you've never before."

"Let the world know if the news isn't common,
That Santa's converted and become a good Mormon.
   Never cease to be merry and full of good cheer,
Merry Christmas to all, and a Happy New Year."

A LETTER TO SANTA CLAUS

Dear Santa:

We understand Walter is going to school,
So maybe some books, pens, paper and rule
   Would help him along in his intellectual soar,
He doesn't seem pleased to pound nails anymore.
   His mind has progressed to a more interesting
      sphere,
I guess we'd be selfish to try keep him here.
   Marlis has talents that are a joy to behold;
As a butterfly's wings we see them unfold.
   She's a dear sweet companion and mother that's
      good
In directing the ways of a sweet brilliant brood.
   She's spiritually growing; we've seen it each year,
An example to all; her testimony sincere.
   She can teach or advise, or wisely direct
In a humble and spiritual way we reflect.
   Upon an improvement she brings to our view
Which to scholars like me was long overdue.
   We can see their young children, amazingly bright
With two languages learned and probably right.
   As far as I know, for I struggle with one
In expressing some thoughts in these lines I have
      done.
   It seems to me, words can hardly express
The feelings we have mixed with joy and distress

When bidding farewell to such loveable friends
And hope that a fond memory of us never ends.
So Santa, we'll turn this mean task over to you;
Keeping track of their needs; administer to them too
And since you're a Mormon; of this we don't
doubt
We're sure the Missionaries ferreted you out
And converted you wholly, without any restraint
Else why are you called a Nicholas Saint?
You'll remember to ask the Lord's help in your
task
In blessing the Jordi's forever, we ask.

(This poem was written in honor of the Jordis' and pre-sented at a farewell party given for them by the Rimbey Branch at the home of Delbert and Betty Purnell near Sylvan Lake. This was near the Christmas season of 1980).

CHRISTMAS IN 1981

Another Yuletide and we see
Many a gorgeous Christmas tree
 And twinkling lights on house and street
And listen to the Carols sweet
 While children wait for Santa Claus
Imagine they hear reindeer paws,
 And sure enough in several stores
During time through shopping chores
 We see this jovial, whiskered man,
All dressed in red and white; again
 Encouraging little ones who'd dare
To climb into his cushioned chair
 And sit upon his lap awhile
To tell him soberly; with dimpled smile
 How very good they've been this year
With hope and faith that he would hear
 And grant each innocent request
Old Santa claims he'll do his best.
 We older folk stand back and grin
And wish that we were young again
 So all that we would need to do
Is wish—and have our wish come true
 With only faith and hope so mild;
Oh! for the faith of a small child!
 Once more we sing the sweet refrain
Of "Peace on Earth, Good Will to Men."

Exchanging gifts with those most dear
Glad for this blessing one more year.
 Still clinging to the hope one day
That prosperous times will come our way,
 We hope that peace on earth will come
To bless the home of everyone
 And none will e'er be forced to bed
Without good food and roof o'erhead.
 May all rejoice because they're free
And live on earth so joyfully.
 We say our prayers when day is done
And pray each day "Bless everyone"
 And feel that we have done our part
Relaxed in praise "How Great Thou Art"
 But we must learn from Him who said
"Faith without works (my child) is dead."
 So I must learn, though painfully
That "peace on earth" begins with me.
 God wisely unlike the wee elf
Won't do for us what we can do for ourselves
 If we want peace on earth be sure
Our own motives are clean and pure.
 Our Savior came to earth so we
Could live with Him eternally.
 If we would follow Him it's clear
There'd be no wars another year.
 Old Satan would have lost the test
And earth from strife would gain a rest.

If we would listen to God's voice
Heed his message, make the choice
To live the life prescribed by Him
We'd need not fear the future grim
But gladly sing the songs of cheer,
A Merry Christmas and Bright New Year!

(This poem was written at the request of Lenore Cahoon, for the Christmas program of 1981. The author used it also for their Christmas letter of 1981. Mary Ann Rompain sent it in to the Rimbey Record. They published it in their paper).

FAITH AND HOPE
(Christmas, 1984)

This Yuletide Greeting comes your way
As Christmas time again has come.
A hopeful message to convey
And wish Godspeed to everyone.

Our "Peace on Earth; Good Will to Men"
Is standard greeting and refrain
'Twas never wished more fervently
Though we're aware with might and mien

That battles rage so mightily
In countries near and countries far;
What meaning has the Christ Child's birth
Proclaimed by angels and the star

When mortals desecrate the earth
And crush the human soul
By their pretense that He is dead
Allowing Satan's fiendish toll

To cause confusion and distress
Thwarting most hopes to win
The human goal to happiness
In a world so steeped in sin?

"Truth crushed to earth will rise again."
God is not mocked nor is He dead.
His kingdom on this earth He'll regain,
And peace on earth will rule again instead.

All wickedness on earth will burn
And righteous mankind will be free
From bondage, hunger, and sojourn
In perfect love and harmony.

Meanwhile we must all do our best
To make life's course complete,
God cannot guide our footsteps
If we refuse to move our feet.

So it is up to each of us, my friend,
To choose life's destiny or fate.
May happiness be ours to win
In a world of love; devoid of hate.

BLESSING OF TIME

Time marches on and once again
We view the Christmas lights,
While politicians struggle in
Decisions for our "human rights."

"Peace on the Earth" is growing dim;
There's turmoil near and far.
Let's cling to hope and follow Him
As Wise Men did the Eastern Star.

We're grateful for the gift of love
He gave to everyone;
The greatest gift sent from above,
His only Beloved Begotten Son.

We're thankful too we have a home
While it is mobile - we are too,
And glad that we are on our own
Ignoring work we used to do.

We hope that every one of you
Enjoy good health and happiness,
And may the Holidays and New Year too
Find you and yours are greatly blessed!

RESPONSIBILITY
(Season's Greetings)

The air is cold and crisp and we
Behold the dazzling Christmas tree,
While merchants try a persuasive plot
To spend our money we "ain't" got.

"No use to worry needlessly
No payments due 'til February"
The gifts so gorgeous we'd love to share
If we were each a millionaire.

But we must settle for just cards
With which to send our best regards.
And hopefully we'll also hear
From friends and loved ones far and near.

Our prayers for them shall ever be
That God will bless them constantly,
Our friends and loved ones are worth more
Than wealth the world is struggling for.

When can they learn to listen to
The message clear to me and you?
As told in scriptures read again
The Prince of Peace was born to reign

On earth; and hate should disappear
At Christmas time and through the year.
This lesson should each one apply:
We shouldn't blame the other guy

But carefully we should look within,
Sure that our own soul unstained by sin
Can deal with all men honestly
With love as we would want to be.

Living the Golden Rule on earth
In honor of the Savior's birth.
Oh! What a glorious world 'twould be
Where peace would reign eternally!

BEST WISHES

(Christmas 1991, Worland, Wyoming)

Best wishes go from us this year
Just like the years before,
To friends and loved ones far and near
Except our love grows even more.

It's hard to think of something new
To make this more exciting,
So we'll just calmly wish for you
God's blessings at this writing.

I suppose Christmas would be drab
Without the usual fuss
Of stringing lights on streets and trees
But it's too strenuous for us.

We slowly rock and reminisce
Of "good old days" gone by;
Tales told devoid of hardships risked
As all those years went creeping by.

We count our blessings often when
We think of all the poor
Who have no shelter, food, and then
Deprived of joys we have galore.

The Christ Child came to live on earth
To teach us charity.
The angels heralded His birth
Though He must die on Calvary.

His gift of love redeemed mankind,
And this projects the reason
We lovingly give gifts and find
Such joy each Christmas season.

Let's carry on the best we can
Each day in life progressing
Toward the goal at our command
And count each one a blessing.

Again we wish much joy to you
At Christmas time, and more
Good times, good health in '92
Than you have had before.

WHY ANN LANDERS

(1992)

We read Ann Landers and we learn
"Christmas news letters" we should spurn.
Those sentiments we do not share
We're glad for news from anywhere.

We hope in turn that you'll find the time
To accept best wishes with this rhyme,
We well may say we've stood the test
Of "Father Time" - and greatly blessed,

We've sufficient strength to do each day
The menial tasks that come our way.
We're mindful of the love that's sent
From friends and neighbors who are bent

On keeping out a "watchful eye"
In making sure we're getting by.
The phone calls too we love to get
From loved ones who just want to let

Us know we're thought of and to say
They wish us well in every way
And then as if that's not enough
They'll just drop in with plates of stuff

Like cakes and cookies, loaves of bread
"Forget the diets; eat instead".
Those words are music to our ears
'Til bathroom scales confirm our fears

Of being overweight and we
Won't look like "slim-jims" on T.V.
We hope good fortune smiles on you
Every day the whole year through

As you proceed in '93
To live your life productively.
As we all know our destiny
Depends on what we strive to be.

May we live worthy of the love
Bestowed on us from Heaven above
Announced by angels of His birth
The Holy Christ Child sent to earth.

He grew from babe to full manhood
Living the way He knew He should;
And later gave His life that we
May live with Him eternally.

MERRY CHRISTMAS AND HAPPY NEW YEAR!

GLORIOUS HERITAGE

The best things in life we are told are all free
But I failed to find any in my shopping spree,
Especially at Christmas time the prices seem high.
I can think of a hundred gifts that I'd like to buy.

If I were as rich as the Wise Men of old
Bearing their precious gifts: myrrh, frankincense,
     gold,
I'd give everyone that I'd ever met
The best Christmas presents they'd ever had yet.

And now a Sweet Spirit whispers something to me:
"Remember you said that the best gifts are free."
The Christ Child was born on that Christmas day
And gave us Salvation in His own special way.

He gave us His own life; on the cross He has paid
To redeem us from Satan. Simple rules He has made.
"Keep my commandments" is all He's required,
"Share with all others talents you have acquired".

"Love one another as I have loved you"
(Even the thoughtless ones who have failed to be
     true)
"Come follow me" is all that it takes
To find your way home; repent of mistakes.

It is no problem to send love as before
To you, and best wishes we're sending galore.
May this Christmas be the best for each one of you
And your New Year be filled with many joyful days
       too.

ACCEPTANCE

(Merry Christmas and Happy New Year!)

We've nothing much to write about
That would excite or interest you
While you are getting stockings out
To hang on fireplace as folks do.

At least we hope you all have socks
And things to put in them
Instead of present hard time knocks
That plague less fortunate of men.

We just don't feel we need much more
Than we've already got,
No fancy things we're yearning for
No place to put them like as not.

Old Santa Claus can take back north
Our stockings full of aches and ills;
Arthritis and old age calls forth
A heating pad and loads of pills.

But as we read the news and see
The human suffering everywhere
We realize we're blessed and we
Find our complaints cannot compare.

So we'll join in at Christmas time
And sing carols in frosty air
In twinkling lights and church bell chimes
That lift our spirits from despair.

The Christ Child will return again
As we've been promised long ago.
With love and hope we should remain
His faithful servants here below.

Until that time keep warm as toast
With food to eat and roof o'erhead
And calls from those you love the most
To cheer and brighten days ahead.

When you have time please write a line
And tell us what you think
Did you enjoy this simple rhyme
Or should I have saved my ink?

A TIME FOR EVERYTHING

Thanksgiving Day has passed us by
While Christmas ushered in
Gets much more notice as we try
To put each date in place again.

Reverently we bow our heads
And thank Him for our blessing
His sacrifice and love for us
Though we can be distressing.

He asks that we help folks in need,
Some means with them to share.
Help "E'en unto one of the least of these"
We show to Him we care.

The Christmas spirit comes as sure
As we bring in the tree,
And try to make it as secure
As we have energy.

With light strings here and tinsel there
And decorations too,
It gradually shows a beauty rare
As we stand back to view.

Now I check on the Christmas list
Of letters and of cards
Regretting all the ones I missed
Last year, with best regards.

A few have gone beyond the veil;
Those we do miss so much,
But to dear ones left we must not fail
To send our love and keep in touch.

We hope that these few lines will say
What we'd like to express:
That you'll enjoy your Christmas day,
And all next year find happiness.

LOST CARDS
(1994)

'Twas not long before Christmas, when all through
    the house
Not a card could I find, and I queried my spouse
To learn if he saw where I stashed them last year
When the season was over and the bargains were
    here.

As I saw them so tempting in every store
I resolved I'd be early next year and before
The rush would engulf me in the mercantile craze
For my very last coin banked in previous days.

Well, I searched Milo's mind but don't ask me why;
He assured me I'd find them by next fourth of July.
So I took out my paper to type a few lines
To greet friends and loved ones and hope they are
    fine.

We're grateful for loved ones, good neighbors, and
    friends,
Each one seems so watchful and promptly attends
To each detail in helping, be the task great or small
And tries to convince us "'twas no trouble at all."

We ask that the Savior, whose birth we revere
Will pour out His blessings as your needs will
     appear.
You remind us that we should remember Him too
As we put Christ in Christmas by the good things we
     do.

FAVORITE THINGS
(1995)

We look forward to receiving the letters
And cards at this time of the year,
That tell us you haven't forgotten
The two ancient people still living here.

We view the excitement of people
As they shop with meticulous care,
They seem to ignore the cold breezes
That ride on the frost laden air.

Many yards and houses are gleaming
With garlands and lights everywhere
While I'm in my rocking chair dreaming
Of days when sweet song birds were here.

I love pretty flowers in baskets
Or in pots, or wherever they be,
But give me green grass and warm sunshine;
Oh, bring back sweet springtime to me!

It is good to remember the Christ Child,
And treasure the gift of "Good News",
But this should be every day lifestyle;
This pattern of life we should choose.

If we will acknowledge His giving
His life spent on cruel Calvary,
His birth would express greater meaning;
He gave life for you and for me.

His handiwork shows in the garden
And every green leaf on the tree,
I hope snow stays up in the mountains;
Oh, bring back sweet summer to me!

MERRY CHRISTMAS (anyway)
and HAPPY NEW YEAR!

LET'S CONSIDER

"World Day of Prayer" we must realize
That people are crying for peace and good will
  Should we question the cause of war clouds that
      rise
Over most of the world; doesn't God love us still?
  Or has He forsaken His children these days
And turned a deaf ear to the prayers we render?
  Isn't He the same God to whom we sing praise
And acknowledge His love is most tender?

Yes, God's in His heaven; All's well with His earth
When we but consider our part in His plan
  By living our lives in the best way we can
In keeping His Covenants, proving our worth
  In placing our values on loftier planes
And serving our sisters and brothers
  Instead of pursuing our own selfish gains
Forever, and disregard others.

How often we long for the old days again
When honor subdued desecration
  And we overcame hardships by laughing at pain
Of long hours of work yielding much satisfaction
  In accomplishments won and an honest night's rest
With no evil deeds plaguing our minds

Secure in the serene, peaceful home we were
      blessed
Nor fear of destruction by vandal's design.

We are prone to remember the fun times we had
And forget many perils we faced
  In pioneer days there were good times with bad
With the bad memories mostly erased.
  Unless the excitement insists they remained
And tend to make heroes with strife
  Like the times when prairie or forest fires claimed
Many acres of crops and threatened our lives.

No murmur of sit down strikes were heard then
But man beside man worked together
  For love of their country and homes were to them
Their reason for honest endeavor.
  The teams in the fields worked from dawn until
      night
As they plowed, planted, harvested too
  The rattle of hay wagons were sounds of delight
The whistle of steam engine summoned the crew.
  The threshers had appetites you couldn't believe
And the wives worked so hard to prepare
  The mounds of fried chicken and food to relieve
The hunger of all working there,
  And I as a child was obliged to refrain
From repast until all men had eaten.

Then after the meal I had to remain,
Until dishes were done; I felt beaten.

Now, how can we profit by past history today
Take a good look; I think that somehow
    You'll see when people forget God and go their
        own way
Thinking they have no use for Him now
    With luxuries and prosperity they build a high wall
Between themselves and God as a rule,
    The higher they build, the greater the fall
Let's turn back to God and don't be a fool.

*(The above poem and the following poem, "I Remember,"
were given by the author in Rimbey, Alberta, on two occasions,
by request, for "World Day of Prayer" programs about 1980 and
1981. The poems were given for different organizations, one for
Senior Citizens and the other at the Church of the United.)*

I REMEMBER

I remember e'er September,
Years ago when I was small
  Children walked to school in country,
Many miles no bus to haul
  Those youngsters to one small building;
They were on their own each day.
  One young lady was the teacher
Forty dollars was her pay.

Slates and double desks were common
Pencils, pens were used but few;
  Ink bottles or wells were tumbled
By braids on girls in front of you.
  Cobs and coal were binned in hallroom
Fuel for stove to keep us warm.
  Mice stole in and chewed our mittens,
Books and papers; and more harm

When mice became so very playful
Scampering around first here, then there
  Making all the children gleeful
When teacher screamed and jumped on chair.
  We were eager to protect her
As we wildly took up chase
  Wielding rulers as deflectors
Finally killed mice in bookcase.

In the early autumn sunshine
Golden shocks were tossed in air
    Filling hayracks pulled to thresher;
Men and teams were everywhere,
    Women hovered stove in kitchen
Cooking up a sumptuous fare
    Mounds of mashed potatoes; chicken
Fried and browned with utmost care.

Children too were running errands
Carrying water, hauling wood
    Each one given special duty
Each one working as one should.
    Stacks of dishes were the burden,
They were washed and dried by some
    Of the young girls; almost ladies,
Soon young wives they would become.

Now the wives and men grown older
"Senior Citizens" are we
    Reminiscing bygone days
We are proud as well we should be
    Of accomplishments we've rendered
And the frontiers we have won.
    Friends and neighbors we've remembered
Worked, played, shared with everyone.

We would not exchange for money
Joys and hardships that we've had
   Maybe "Good Old Days" weren't funny
But we now can say we're glad.
   Our experiences were teachers;
Teaching lessons of great worth
   In appreciating blessings
We now have upon the earth.

We are glad to join in praying
Uniting in "World Day of Prayer"
   Confident that God is hearing
Prayers for Peace and He does care.
   Now the world must learn His bidding
Each must learn the Master's Art
   Loving neighbors and forgiving
From the bottom of each heart.

YESTERDAY, TODAY AND TOMORROW

Dear mothers and daughters
  Of God's chosen flock.
Let's pretend for a while
  We can turn back the clock
To only a moment we'll call yesterday
  When primary daughters
Were captured from play
  And brought to His house
In the wisest of schemes,
  To grow in the Gospel while tiny Sunbeams
You were radiant and active
  And it just seems that we
Find no church members more active
  Than those little cherubs aged three.
And you became Stars
  At the years four and five.
You still were so precious
  And much more alive.
At ages six and seven you were ever so bright,
  Your ambition both years
Were designed "Choose the Right."
  And then as you grew
Into more formative years
  Your aims were still higher
As "A" and "B" Targeteers."
  You've moved to today
And it's easy to see

You're becoming so lovely
As a "Merrie Miss A and B."
You are growing so fast
You're soon out of today
As you advance into "B"
From the class we call "A."
Patricia, Sandy, Cheryl, and Colleen,
What good little workers
In your group you have been!
You'll be seniors in Primary
And shoulder the load
Of examples e'er set in live the code
"It will radiate the light of the Gospel
From the days of my early life,"
You will rejoice with the Lord
As you overcome strife.
Farewell Tammy, Denise, Julie, Sue Ann
As you walk into tomorrow
We're sure than you can
Make "good" even "better"
And the "better" make "best"
In the Mutual Improvement
As you grow with the rest.
Your Primary teachers and mothers will pray
You'll uphold the standards
You learned yesterday
Your lofty ideals are always in style
They'll ever be helpful

And very worthwhile
As tomorrow you journey
  In life's devious ways
Holding dear to the truths
  Learned in your yesterdays,
Through high school and college.
  And some day may you choose
A companion who is good
  And is worthy of you,
That you'll be united
  In the temple of the Lord
Where you will be blessed
  By obeying His word.
And away into tomorrow
  Very remotely it's true
Your own little daughters
  Will be smiling at you.
Because you learned well
  From the past, don't you see
The best place to start
  Is with Mother in Church Primary.

(Written at the request of Sister Zelda Corbett).

TRIBUTE TO RELIEF SOCIETY

A Prophet in this dispensation
Was admonished by the Lord
To establish an organization
To operate in every Ward.

So the Relief Society came into function
To administer to th' poor and th' sick
And the sisters were to work in conjunction
With the heads of the Bishopric.

The spirit grew swiftly like fire
From pioneer times to our own
And now we may justly admire
The sisters' good work in our town.

Good leaders in our Ward were ne'er wanting,
Since Relief Society came into being,
The incessant labor and talents
Were resplendent in our good Sister Gheen.

Her untiring efforts paid dividends
As she worked both early and late,
Six years she worked as our president
Beginning in 1928.

The needle and fancy work flourished
As they canvassed L.D.S. homes in their car.
Holding meetings, encouraging ladies to
Bring their best work to the Bazaar.

The articles sold up in Lovell
Would help in the Church Building Fund,
While others decorate their homes
With the fancy work the sisters had done.

Ludina Whitlock became leader
Her years in this office were eight;
She engineered fund raising projects
And sent the first delegates to Salt Lake.

The Building Fund also expanded,
Each shoulder was placed at the wheel.
They sent in the first $80.00 —
The hope for a Chapel was real.

Sylvia Nielson stepped forward in duty
Her ingenuity can't be ignored;
She discovered the way to men's purses
Thru the medium of the famed Smorgasbord.

The sisters were challenged by brethren
Who thought they could keep in their pace;
Six years found them barely succeeding
'Twas a grueling, enjoyable race.

Virginia Kimzey next came in her order
The preceding pattern to enhance
Resolved in her aim like the others
The House of the Lord to advance.

Marion Nielson, and then Maggie Tolman
Served as presidents respectively stated,
Contributed much, as well each one can
And the sisters were greatly elated.

To be able to meet in the House of the Lord
Brother Benson had just dedicated
Receiving the blessings, obey the word
Upon which these are all predicated.

Elva Cook was the next leader selected;
Another good Latter-day Saint.
By this time you've probably expected
The work was all done, but don't faint.

The membership now has most doubled;
There's plenty of labor to do.
Don't try to hide talents, nor shuttle
They're sure to find out if you do.

Marge Owens and her counselors were summoned
To accept the call in this Ward
Of Relief Society leaders
Ordained by the hand of the Lord.

Their "Church Wagon" dinners were luscious;
The team work was evident there,
As with similar projects they were sponsored
Each one planned with meticulous care.

Maxine Lowe drove up in the mountains
Hoping for time to relax,
But the Bishops employed their detectives
And requested she retrace her tracks.

Seriously now, I am speaking
Don't think this a pretense of jest
The Lord knows whom He is seeking
He always chooses the best.

Maxine, who now holds the honor
Of President, I'm sure you agree
Magnifies the call placed upon her
In her cherished Relief Society.

Let's join with the sweet Singing Mothers
That we have so often enjoyed,
To thank the Heavenly Father
For the servants He wisely employed.

There are many names that weren't mentioned
I beseech you, my faults overlook
No offense have I ever intended
And the Lord has your name in His Book.

ENDEARING ENDEAVORS
(1993)

God gave us life and the gift of His Son
To redeem us and prove that He loves everyone.
He created the heavens; He created the earth;
Such exquisite beauty! He gave all creatures birth.

Except for old Satan and his angels at war
Who rebelled against principles Heavenly Father
     stood for.
Free agency to mortals Satan would have denied
And demanded God's glory to savor his pride.

Elohim in His wisdom rejected that plan
And accepted the one wherein everyone can
Choose for herself the way she would go
With the Spiritual Light to direct here below.

Each sister is special! And each one is given
At least one fair talent to take back to heaven,
If she will just magnify and create with all care
The best that she can and with others will share.

So Sisters, enjoy and be uplifted too
By the love that is felt in good things that you do.
This truth must you know - the writer's amazed
At the talents expressed in multitudinous ways.

An attempt to list all would boggle the mind.
But as I look around I can't help but find
Inspirations galore that seem so far outreaching
So thanks to you sisters for your examples and
        teaching

How to create with the talents acquired,
Through our prayers and efforts we're truly inspired.
You remind us that we each have so much to give;
It is ours to respond well as long as we live.

(Written by request to complement a Relief Society lesson.)

A TRIBUTE TO SISTER ORA CANNON

This tribute to you we would now like to pay
A woman so noble, so good, and so true
For all you have done in your own sweet way
The whole Worland Ward is indebted to you.

With diligence and faith you always have worked
So the Church can function much better
Your call to service you never have shirked
In preparing and sending our News Letter.

The little children all love you so
As they around you hover
In Kindergarten, Sunday School, Primary, or Home
Because you're their darling teacher or mother.

You've truly embarked in the service of God
And He has answered your prayer
Your family has clung to the great "iron rod"
In fulfilling their missions with care.

So quiet and humble you go on your way
Never asking for special attention
Your sacrifices you place on your altar each day
Without as much as a mention.

Each day you're a sermon in faith and in deeds
Encouraging and guiding your brothers
Sharing and giving according to needs;
A living example for others.

Again we say "Thank You" for all you have done
And for the future, "Many Thanks" more
May we all take heed from the example you've
shown
That we in the Gospel may be more secure.

TRUE TO OUR CALLING
(1985)

Be mindful that you are a child of God;
Don't underrate your worth,
Your mission consider with high regard
In determining achievement on the earth.

Serve righteously though it may seem hard to do,
Do your best during each precious hour
To lighten the burdens of others, pursue
With help in wisdom from Heavenly power.

Be true to all those who trust you;
True friends may bolster your life.
"E'en as ye do it unto one of the least of these"
Can bring you happiness; avoid strife.

Self discipline is more than self control,
Its value each one should rate
In propelling toward a loftier goal,
Don't under-estimate.

It doesn't take talent to act stupid
And drift like dumb cattle at night;
It is one of strong character who is willing
To concede the petty skirmish and win the significant
       fight.

It may seem great to conquer a city
In the struggle to gain affluent wealth,
But Oh! How much greater the pity
When one fails to control one's own self.

There's nothing noble in being superior to any
        other man (woman)
As an old Hindu proverb tells,
The true nobility is in being
Superior to one's former self.

There's no disgrace in failure
Unless you fail to try.
Seek out the lesson to be learned
Ennobling your character by and by.

Entertain uplifting thoughts;
"Hitch your wagon to a star."
What you think about when you don't have to think
Proves what you really are.
It's not what you get but more what you give;
Not just what you say, but more how you live,
Forgetting yourselves in service to others;
These are the attributes of good Latter-day Saint
        sisters and brothers.

Written by request of sister Priscilla Ferris of Thermopolis; Feb. 26, 1985, to be used for distribution at General Womens' Fireside from S.L. (March 3rd).

THE MORMON TRAIL

Across the State o'er hills and vales
Are found some deep and hard worn trails,

Ground by the souls of yester-years
Known as the "Mormon Pioneers."

Their testimony cannot fail
To prick our hearts; in their travail.

They bore some loved ones to their graves
Along the way: still they were brave

In doing what they felt they should
In keeping sacred as God would

The covenants they made with Him
Though death seemed sure and life was grim,

But knowing well that this must be
A test for all eternity.

Life is at best of short duration
While working out his own salvation.

Each one by careful training knows
Through service to the Lord he grows

In faith from youth to endless time
In sun, in rain, in fun, in grime.

The darkest night will meet the light of dawn
Hardships strengthen souls to carry on

Their mission in this life however spent
Must be to know the one true God and Jesus Christ
            whom He has sent.

Thanks be to God forevermore
For brave men who have gone before

Who nobly fought for all that's good
And sealed their testimonies with their blood.

That all might learn that God can feel
And not intangible, but real.

He does not send to hell, your soul
Where Satan stirs eternal coal

If you have died deprived still
Of the true Gospel and God's will.

"Truth crushed to earth will rise again"
Born to the light by noble man.

"Let freedom ring" was meant for me
Earned by the sons of liberty.

In history, to cite just one
Dear valiant soul, Tom Jefferson

Ordained of God, premortally
To gain for men free agency

In this great land of choice creation
A forerunner of the Restoration

Of the true Gospel of the Lord.
The way was long, the fight was hard.

Freedom of religion, Independence of mankind
Intelligence and education of the mind.

Slavery abolished was his goal
Men are created equal; men's minds and soul

Should not be shackled, and no less
May politicians hinder speech or press.

Great were his adversities, fearless were his fights
While Madison was prevailed upon to add the Bill of
        Rights.

By the influence and persuasion of Thomas Jefferson
Who bought Louisiana Territory from sad Napoleon

For fifteen million was the price
Jefferson's opponents were not nice

In names they called and "bricks" they threw
As he "violated the Constitution;" this he knew.

But he persisted and what's more
He sent Lewis and Clark out to explore,

And make some maps of where they'd been
Reporting everything they'd seen.

In later years the Saints acquired
These same reports and maps required

By former companies to make;
Seeming to be just for their sake.

For if the promptings of the Lord had failed
Postponed would be that Mormon trail.

The Gospel fair could not have thrived
If freedoms had not been revived

By hands of wise men of the Lord
Redeemed as with His own accord

To keep the promises of old
In Bible times they were foretold.

Jefferson seemed to be endowed
With discernment of the Clergy's fraud.

They branded him an "atheist" while he bore true by
      revelation
A testimony with elation.

"The genuine and simple religion of Jesus will be
      restored
Such as it was preached and practiced by the Lord."

God bless those souls who did not fail
To stand the test; to blaze the trail

That we may live and blessed be
Choice spirits in eternity.

WITH LOVE TO BISHOP ALLRED

Over near Lovell on a hot summer day
A stork was seen flapping his lone weary way.
He landed at Mary and Bert Allred's place
With a bundle from heaven, now called "Outer
      Space".

Yes, he landed at Allred's on the day July 1,
When the twentieth century its sixth year had begun.
The baby was tired, but he let out a yell
That told this young couple he had come there to
      dwell.

His feet were quite long and his face was so red;
He hadn't much hair on the top of his head.
But his parents exclaimed, "What a beautiful son
This Allred infant is our own John Leland!"

We've come here to honor this great handsome man
For the life he has lived and pray that he can
Continue his sense of good humor and wit
And make this world brighter for the sharing of it.

Bishop Allred step forward; This is your life.
Later, we'll ask you to present your wife.
We've made these arrangements and hope you don't
      fuss
If we just try to tell you what you mean to all of us.

We've checked with your family and dug into books;
Snooped into each cranny and some remote nooks.
Your records have proved what we've all realized
You're a man of great talent and much enterprise.

From Lovell you moved with your mother and dad
And your sister and brothers to the farm your folks
    had
On the Nowood near Ten Sleep so we heard the folks
    say
On the old "Redland Farm" they decided to stay.

Well farm it they did as farm it they ought
For this was the home that your family bought.
Mosquitoes were pesky and working days long;
But in spite of hard knocks you all got along.

You didn't have buses to haul you to school;
So self education was often the rule.
Young Leland you learned to spell, cipher, and write,
And many a lesson you worked by lamp light.

On through high school you went with your books
        and your pen;
Then more correspondence you tackled again
Until you accomplished with much dedication
A knowledge of electricity and refrigeration.

From the Conservatory of Music in Honolulu so far
You earned a teacher's certificate playing the
      Hawaiian guitar.
Lillian remembers when square dances were tops;
Young Leland was playing for Old Timer's hops.

The music was lively and the dancers were too,
And the time was nearly morning before they got
      through.
They didn't need liquor nor drugs nor that stuff;
Just a new rural teacher was exciting enough.

Young Allred advanced and was never outdone;
At the Otter Creek School he was second to none.
He spent so much time there with Rachel we see
She was persuaded to get her MRS. degree.

In the year '36 on the 12th day of June
Lee and Rachel set out for their life's honeymoon,
Dr. John Roberts in his mission renown
United this couple in his best cap and gown.

And so they were married and Leland could tell
Rachel couldn't start fires with green wood very well
So soon he discovered this young wife he must spoil;
He bought her a stove that functioned on oil.

Their home was as cozy as most log houses were
      then,
There was dirt on the roof that kept the warmth in
When winter was chilly; or in summer 'twas cool;
On most days the "temp" was just right as a rule.

The water Lee hauled from the Nowood hard by;
And I guess that's what prompted "Here's mud in
      your eye."
The plumbing(?) was outdoor and considered real
      neat
Except in the winter when frost's on the seat.

Then Mary Ann came in May '37
And Rachel said, "Leland, city life would be
      heaven."
To Worland they moved in the year '38
And made them a home that was really first rate.

"Now this is like living," his Rachel went on
So they straitly prepared for their new baby John.
In the very next year on October the 4th,
You could hear Leland shout from the south to the
      north.

"It's a boy! It's a boy!" He yelled long and loud,
And you never did see a young daddy more proud.
Their family grew up as young families do,
Bringing joy with achievement and grandchildren
      too.

And during these years there was no time to dream.
A business was built by a "plumbing" good team.
There was Leland and Ellis both working like mad
To prosper in plumbing with the small start they had.

Ellis Allred went west as some young couples will,
But Leland, his plumbing he worked with all skill.
So as the years prospered, the Allreds they grew
Instead of one business they now managed two.

There was one on North 9th that was big and grand
Made of white gypsum blocks; Lee had built it by
      hand.
The other was purchased at Lovell from Card.
With Leland as owner and Charles Wittick in charge.

To keep up with Leland in his work is a chore,
For he's out of one thing into two dozen more.
He had a drag line and then did more plumbing,
Then in carpenter work he was right up and coming.

He built a big house of some 13 room space;
And this dwelling was super at 508 Grace.
Lee found enough time to build yet another;
An apartment of three rooms to provide for his
      mother.

Their children grew up as I told you before;
And their folks didn't need this big house anymore.
But this was no problem for a family so skilled.
They promptly proceeded a new house to build

In the Nissen Addition and a hard one to beat;
It was all ultra modern with radiant heat.
And a farm was acquired by a deal that Lee made
For the big house in town that was given in trade.

And all of this time there were plans taking root
To channel this couple where more talents would suit
To work for the Lord so their spirits could grow
As tall as their minds and reach up as they go.

To Celestialized Glory the records all say
What tremendous strides they have taken this way.
Lee's spark was rekindled and "sure" came alive,
Owen Evert made him an Elder in the year '55.

So true to their faith as the Prophet revealed
On their 21st Anniversary their marriage was sealed.
Lee kept right on moving as High Priest and Ward
      Clerk,
Then on in the Bishopric Leland did work.

He was chosen First Counselor as most of us know,
To help in the office of Bishop Ray Lowe.
But Bishop Lowe's health forced an early release;
Bishop Allred was chosen and given the keys

By authority given as the Church should be run
At that time the Stake President was Glen E. Nielson,
And now as a matter of Ward history
Our new Bishop was sustained in the year '63.

His Counselors too were both chosen through prayer;
David Asay and Gene Whitlock in the Bishopric
      share.
As time drifted on and one was released,
Scott Paris soon found that his duties increased.

Later on when Gene Whitlock asked permission to
      go,
They conveniently latched on to our Brother Max
      Lowe.
Then there's Maurice Cannon who has done faithful
      work
Keeping the books as our official Ward Clerk.

While all these good brethren were serving our Ward
They built an addition to the House of the Lord.
So many good times we can remember quite well,
But the sleep that was lost only the leaders can tell.

Just a few of their small chores we might mention
        herein;
Are to account for finances that they hope to take in
To help the poor people less fortunate than we
Or to keep the church warm when there's a cold
        tendency.

Then there's Susie and Johnny who want marriage
        vows said,
And countless are times when Bishop is called out of
        bed
To administer to those who are sick in the night
Or settle a quarrel or prevent a big fight.

In case you might yearn for a leisurely walk
You're gently reminded you must give the next talk.
When someone's forgotten an assignment or two
You find these small tasks have just fallen to you.

You can't take a bath unless Rachel's at home
For some one must answer that blamed telephone.
It might be the President of the whole Big Horn
        Stake
Who insists that percentages are quite underweight.

Or the Relief Society might call to complain
That the plumbing downstairs is flooding again.
What with welfare and tithing and finances too
And cheering the people who so often feel blue.

And advising and counseling, coordinating and then
Check the windows and doors and the lighting again.
We wonder why sometimes you're looking quite
      glum
You live like a king, you're so serious - how come?

The Ministerial Society has set you a date
To meet with these men you evaluate
The progress you make with community teams
In spreading the Gospel and fulfilling your dreams.

You've served seven years and we have been blessed
With Rachel behind you you've both done your best,
And we think the good Lord would be long on His
      praise
But He hasn't yet turned you to pasture to graze.

Keep right in there pitching, may your progress
      increase
With your wit and your wisdom, and on bended
      knees
We'll pray that you're happy in the work of the Lord
As you bless many souls in the Father's vineyard.

TRIBUTE TO BISHOP ROBERT PARIS

Up through the valley of life in our time
Flow memories of many indelibly entwined
Of friendships; of loved ones whom we have met.
Reminiscing life's moments we'll never forget.

Many are old friends and some are quite new,
Each contributing joy that we fondly renew.
Robert Paris was reared in this Worland superb
By goodly parents: dear Helen and Herb.

Three brothers and two sisters influenced him,
Scott, Charles, and Mark, and Kay, and Lynn
Until Robert left home, more confidence grew,
Progressing academically in the renowned BYU.

More progress was made fulfilling a dream
When he won Jeanie Gorst, his sweetheart and
     queen.
He became a good dentist, husband and dad
And thought that a large family wouldn't be bad.

But Jeanie declared that Bob's idea of heaven
Was far too advanced, so they settled for seven.
Jacqueline, Gretchen, and Jason, then Sara and Ann,
With Martha and Jessica at the end of the clan.

We're tempted to think that with this little crew,
That Jeanie and Robert had all they could do.
But what we might think doesn't always count with
      the Lord,
As Robert was ordained father of Worland First
      Ward.

Scott Smith, a member of the Stake Presidency
Ordained Bishop Paris, 9 November, 1980.
Larry Coppock was ordained a High Priest the same
      day
And became the first counselor in a similar way.

Jerry Kienlen was called second counselor there
To work in the Bishopric, the challenge to share.
The Bishop and counselors did their duty and more
Until the counselors were released in 1984.

Max Bessinger and Mike Snyder were made
      counselors then,
Robert Akin made it plain they were capable men.
Stake Presidents have habits that seem almost like
      tricks,
They released all the Bishopric in 1986,

Except the clerk, who is known as John Dent,
He remains to take charge of the money that's spent.
He has worked in this office since '81 or '82,
A good-natured guy, and a quiet one, too.

Don Harris served also as a Ward Clerk,
His records and accounts show he too did good work.
We hope you don't deem these statistics a bore,
We aren't through applauding, there is a lot more.

In case you've forgotten, we'll remind you again
There's a very good wife helping her famous man.
There's Jeanie, Kaye, Carol, and sweet Mary Sue,
Karla, Sharon, and Clarlyn to name just a few.

We love them, and bless them for the good work they
        have done,
But remember, remember, they have only begun.
In the service of One, our true and supreme Friend,
Each one must continue and endure to the end.

BIRD'S EYE VIEW OF THE BISHOPRIC
(and THIS FIRST WARD)

Narrator: Scene 1

The Bishop is calling by phone from his office his counselors and financial clerk to a special meeting in an effort to reactivate members of the Church. Bishop Paris has given much thought and prayer to this problem. He has an inspiration for the solution, but wishes to seek an affirmation and spiritual insight of his counselors and officers of the Bishopric. This meeting is to be brief - not to exceed three hours duration. (Large clock in background; someone turns hands to indicate passing of time.)

Max Bessinger, Mike Snyder, and John Dent appear at the Bishop's office breathlessly to demonstrate their dedication to the service of the Lord. The Bishop welcomes the counselors and with his huge door key, immediately locks the door to make sure that everything is kept in strict confidence. The problem is again announced (card is held up "Reactivate Members" written on it). Everyone is given sheets of paper upon which to write their inspirations.

Mike Snyder has a rope with which he represents his idea. He feels that lassoing members away from TV's, recreation areas, etc., is the only sure way to bring

137

members back to Church. A few minutes pass and Mike's idea is vetoed. The Bishopric concentrates again. Max Bessinger offers a handful of candy. This indicates the idea that sweet talk should bring about the desired results.

Each one thinks and thinks about this suggestion and is later voted down. Again they are required to think of a solution and go into deep concentration.

John Dent raises his hand to indicate he has an idea. He produces some money from his money bag and suggests that members could be reactivated by offering prizes for attending. Consideration is given and John's idea is also vetoed.

More deep thought and no results. It is concluded that no workable ideas have been extracted from their own efforts and thought. The Lord is sought through prayer. Each one bows in the attitude of prayer.

After a few minutes of prayer each one takes a sheet of paper and writes one word. The Bishop asks for their answers and compares it with his own. They are all the same - the word is LOVE. The Bishop holds up a large red heart indicating their new and continued resolve to win all the inactive members back with increased love. President Asay approved the resolution and commitment with a caution that demonstration is extended at arm's length. Moderation in all things - or avoid the appearance of evil. Let your love be Godly and spiritual.

-Curtain Closes -

* * *

Narrator: Scene 2

We do feel the love of the Bishopric and detect the Bishop's love of God through nature. He loves to go bird watching for relaxation from the strains of ordinary demands.

Even against his better judgment he has gone out alone and wanders into unfamiliar territory. Finally he realizes he is lost. He becomes exhausted and to the point of delirium. He calls out for water, water, WATER. He continues wandering and becomes staggery and finally falls down completely exhausted but still faintly calling for w-a-t-e-r.

Finally, someone who has come along his way offers the Bishop a container of water. The Bishop is so grateful and immediately locates his toothbrush and begins frantically brushing his teeth.

- Curtain Closes -

Narrator: Scene 3

    The Bishopric, still laboring under the stress and strain of solving problems pertaining to spiritual and temporal matters, has composed a new theme song:

THIS FIRST WARD

This First Ward sure keeps us busy
This First Ward sure makes us hop,
First we find ourselves with three jobs
Then a fourth one, like as not.

President Asay says "Keep busy"
Then you'll have no time for sin.
We just ain't got time for nothin'
In this hectic rush we're in.

- chorus -

Ain't gonna need my house no longer,
Ain't gonna need my house no more.
Ain't got time to fix the shingles,
Ain't got time to fix the floor.

Ain't got time to eat no supper
Or to even change my shirt.
Ain't got time to use the toothbrush
'Cause I'm always at the church.

* * *

This old brain's sure gettin' muddled,
This old head's sure gettin' gray,
I taught Courtship and it's hazards
In Primary the other day.

I showed the Ensigns and the Laurels
Just how to make a chair.
And the Elders got the lesson
How to curl and backcomb hair.

- Chorus -

Ain't gonna need my house no longer
I'm gonna try and rent it out.
Ain't got time to fix the windows
Ain't got time to fix the spout.

Ain't got time to mend my britches
Or to make a batch of bread.
Ain't been runnin' up the light bill
Use the Church's lights instead.

* * *

This quartette she sure is feeble
This old choir sure got the shakes.
This old chorus sure lacks something
Just ain't got what all it takes.

The soprano sure is sufferin'
The alto needs a nurse.
The old tenor she is awful
And the bass is even worse.

- Chorus -

Ain't gonna sing this song no longer
Ain't gonna torment you no more.
We're a goin' out the window
'Fore you throw us out the door.

If you'd like to hear it over
You won't even have to search,
Just you come and ask politely,
We'll be right back here in church.

LEAVING HOME

Did Heavenly Parents shed a tear
When earthbound you departed?
Did they show any signs of fear
Or seem to be down hearted?

Or were they like your parents here
Whose advice you're loathe to take?
You'd much prefer your life to live
And make your own mistakes.

Then when you're old the same advice
You freely give and as you try
To guide your youth who seem unwise
And unlike you, you wonder why.

How late we learn wisdom at last
Sometime that flows from pen or tongue
We should improve upon the past
And learn the better way when young.

Your challenge is to find the way
To be a sovereign child of God.
Improve your mind and soul each day;
Cling to the "Iron Rod."

Don't be a conformist to please the crowd;
The majority should not always win.
They crucified our Lord and allowed
The Christians to be fed to lions thin.

The majority persecuted Jews
And captured slaves to use for toil.
The reign of terror fills the news
And martyred Prophets stain the soil.

Opinions of others should be heard
But they're not to be your master.
Stand up, be counted, lest your word
Left silent could prove disaster.

Believe in God, your country and yourself;
In that order, and be sure
When freedom is at stake
Your stand for goodness is secure.

There's no disgrace in failure
Unless you fail to try.
Seek out the lesson to be learned,
Enriching experience by and by.

Accept changes as long as they're for better;
Ruts are just graves with the ends removed.
Most people who miss the boat in life
Failed to chart their course it's proved.

This is the law and the law shall run
'Til the earth in its course stands still
That "He that eateth another's bread
Shall do the others will."

Mouse traps furnish free cheese within
But the mouse's happiness, I have a hunch,
Is very short lived; for mice like men
Find there's no such thing as a free lunch.

Natural talents wasted is a crime.
Everyone can excel at something that is sure.
Anybody can be somebody sometime
With determination, confidence, self reliance; feel
     secure.

"There's nothing noble in being superior to some
     other man"
An old Hindu proverb tells
That true nobility is in being
Superior to your former self.

Accept these words and know we love you,
Every blessing from God we implore
To keep you safe, clean and pure always;
It's our prayer for each one evermore.

We bid you farewell and so fondly
Remember each dear smiling face;
Exchanging your love for the love we give
You'll have made this earth a better place.

(In the spring of 1979 when Angela Rompain, Laurie Purnell, and Michael Wettstein were leaving Rimbey, Alberta L.D.S. Branch, the author was asked to write a poem for their farewell party. "Leaving Home" was the result of that request).

DEAR JANE

(Aug. 15, 1980)

Dear Jane,

We hope you'll remember that we love you too,
And pray for God's blessings in all that you do.
There's a sob in our heart as we bid you farewell
As you reach for the future; your aspirations fulfill.
Take a long look at your values as you go on life's
      way
That still will be with you at life's closing day.
Should you follow the road that leads toward fame,
Or strive after wealth or honorable name?
Should you follow the crowd to the houses of mirth,
Or grope for the product that comes from the earth?
Could you pause in your rush to lighten the load
Of some weary travelers who has a rough road,
To give a kind word - a true, honest smile?
These are the values you'll prize after while.

If life's truest values were honor or wealth,
Or high education, or sound, perfect health,
Good luck or good fortune or prestige galore
Most of us would be barred from entering the door.
It's not what you get but more what you give,
Not just what you say, but more how you live.

Forgetting yourself in your service to others
Like the lullaby song you have heard from your
    mother.
Just to ease someone's burden and cause her to smile.
These are the values you'll prize after while.

When you look at the ocean or look at the sod,
Oh, how can you help but give credit to God?
The tints of the rainbow, the light on the cloud
Oh, how can the spirit of mortal be proud?
The song of the bird is as God's voice
Telling thee to be kind to each soul and deal honestly
And walk with the Saviour on life's rugged road,
Stay near Him and He lightens your load
As you make every journey in life with a smile.
Oh, these are the values you'll prize after while.

Don't forget us, We love you.

*(To Jane Rompain at her farewell party in her parents'
home at Bluffton, Alberta).*

SOME RIMBEY BRANCH MISSIONARIES

Elder Widmer arrived from Idaho State
In Rimbey, his mission to fill.
He thought all the members he met first rate
And eager to help in his efforts - until
He encountered a difficult gal in his rounds.
Rebellious, and set in her ways
Who wouldn't endorse all his plans; he was bound
To involve even Seniors in their latter days.
But as time progressed she felt to repent
Though reluctant to do so at first
Influenced by Widmer that all should repent
And judge not, lest they might be cursed.

Elder Widmer prepared for his Mission real neat
With dark suits of wool, tall fur hat on his head
That he wore in the day but at night on his feet
To help keep him warm in his bed.
That was really a rickety cot of some kind
Which was borrowed along with the rest
Of furnishings gleaned from members who find
Some are poor, some better; some best.
Tribulations increased with a housekeeping chore
Cooking and shopping - no fun
Washing dishes, laundry, mending - a bore
But it helped to budget the "mon",

Elder Styles helped with lessons that Yankees should
        know
Is the proper Canadian way
In asking a question; the best manners show
You don't end with a "huh?" but an "eh?"
Elder Minsker; the top of a house is a roof instead
Of ruff on a howse and what's more
You should know alphabets end with a zed
And you take off your shoes at the door.
You sit on a Chesterfield - don't light one up
As you've seen some Americans do
Don't wipe off your beak with the back of your cuff
But with a serviette handed to you.

Elder Minsker, you brought Elder Widmer good luck
So much that he hardly could speak
His new abode rented and now he could chuck
The old things; he promptly was transferred next
        week
To another more fruitful field he must go
Where his efforts might double in speed
He took with him memories of good times and so
They'd buoy up his spirits indeed.
He'd remember the time of his pulling contest
When with girls he was pulling broomsticks
And he'd blush to confess the girls were best
It must have been feminine tricks.
You were really "far out" like little lost sheep
Stuck in country somewhere and somehow

Refuge was found and you'd now like to sleep
Again in that stable, up in the hay mow.
The driving techniques of some Elders were wild
While trying to see through the ice
To say they were reckless is putting it mild
The bashed Mission Home Truck surely looked nice,
And ditches are scarred around Rimbey as well;
Faith in miracles you can revise
But has anyone ever been able to tell
Where in the world you were taught how to drive?

A bicycle's even a menace to you
In Calgary, so goes the tale
The "Look Mom, No hands!" stunt you never
    outgrew
You tried on the one Crow Foot Trail.
You stooped as you laughed and felt a great draught
For all you had taken your chance
You then realized with tears in your eyes
You had worn out the seat of your pants.
A beautiful suit Widmer purchased with care
He looked sharp and a sight to be seen!
Authorities sternly disapproved that he wear
That color of such a bright green.

Authorities also have an uncanny knack
Of tracking you down if you bend
Just one simple rule: if you fail to get back
At one thirty at night - oops - make it ten.

Well, all right, its a true Gospel, they're sure
And the truth of it they'll sadly declare
That it bugs them to death to have to endure
The wearing of crazy short hair.
They can't wait 'til they're home and do as they
     please
Free agency they'll surely show
But never were times more joyful than these
They'll never more happiness know.

And once they return home they'll hurry right back
To the friends they have made by the score
And maybe a farmer girl one will attract
So he won't have to leave anymore.
Now the Rimbey Branch members are long on their
     praise
In spite of our jesting in fun
Of a couple of Elders we'll remember always
For their kindness and good work they've done.
Elder Minsker was willing to help milk a cow
So the Leitheads could join with the rest
To the temple in Cardston, and therein allow
To work to help others progress.
Elder Minsker did baby sit at the Cahoons'
When the parents felt they could be risky
And on Wettstein's piano he'd pound out a tune
They decided he's no Paderewski.
At siding and roofing he's way out of sight
He works with the greatest of skill

At Cahoon's or at Hopper's he does it up right
To avoid a disastrous spill.
He carefully works with a rope tied around
His body with utmost care
Unless confused gravity gets his head down
And his feet sticking up in the air.

He throws a mean ball on the basketball floor
A basket he makes every time
But the strangest of all is the way he can score
A sun tan with liquid sunshine.
He seems to have methods to work out his scheme
This dashing and dapper young Elder
His tanning just happened by unnatural means
When he tried out his good friend's arc welder.
One gymnastic fete that I'll bet can't be beaten
The Elders when dinner you call
They say its no fun just to eat and then run
But it's better than not eating at all.

The Missionaries earned every bite that they ate
Even though they are artists at stuffing
They don't ask for pay, so don't under rate
They're just - being good - good for nothing.
His mother admonished Miles Minsker, "Forsake
This idea of Canada Bound
Young man it is time your life you must find
And consider just settling down."

"I know you are right, Mother dear and I might
Just consider your advice very sound
I very much fear if I wait one more year
I can't find me a wife that's not found."

Good hunting, dear lads, we wish you Godspeed
And we pray as you journey through life
God's blessings will guide you and fulfill every need
To sustain you through sunshine or strife
You were true to your call, and gallantly you
Can be true to yourself and the Lord.
The Gospel is true; Be aware of this too
That we love you with all sweet accord,
Endure to the end and may we meet again
On the farmlands of Heaven above
With plenty of sunshine and just enough rain
To mature all our efforts with love.

TO MICHAEL WETTSTEIN

A missionary he has grown to be;
   We do so honor him
So clean and pure and wise is he
   And eager to begin
The work the Lord admonishes
   Each one of us to do
In rendering our services
   Is worth endeavor too.

Our Michael goes to Switzerland
   A home land of his dad
Who came from there, we understand
   When he was but a lad.
I can't help being envious
   Of you, young Mike, it's true,
I wonder what would become of us
   If you were me, and I were you.

I'm sure its best that you should go,
   My French would be a mess
The Lord has chosen best I know
   In sending you, I must confess.
So what I'll be content to do
   Is keep the home fires burning
And maybe send advice to you
   'Til time for your returning.

Conjecturing your just appeal
   In all your return dockets
Is "put your shoulder to the wheel
   And get off your hip pockets."
That missionary zeal of Mike's
   Can be some powerful stuff
I'll guess they've never seen the likes
   'Til Authorities say he's done enough.

He's a chip off the old block you bet
   He knows what he's been sent for
The question all the Swiss will get,
   "Would you and you like to know more?"
We hope his patience won't expire
   Or his endurance won't grow thin
Before some kind soul will inquire
   "Won't Missionaries please come in?"

The test is yours; you cannot lose
   Unless you fail to try - but we
Are sure that you would always choose
   To serve the Lord most valiantly.
"Six days a week the devil works
   And overtime on Sunday
And then he's ready once again
   To start anew on Monday.
So if you'd keep your conscience clear
   And stay right on the level

You must begin at early dawn
   And work just like the devil."

I don't know who wrote those eight lines
   It's often made me wonder,
He said it well in fitting rhymes
   So thought I'd steal his thunder.

Remember every soul must hear
   Each soul must have a chance
To embrace the Gospel and adhere
   To principles and thus advance.
Or some may choose to turn away
   Your message cast aside
Each has his own free agency,
   Regardless of how hard you tried.

Give every day the best you can
   The Lord will guide you through
If you will give your all to Him
   He'll give all He has to you,
Trials and tribulations are bound to come
   To test every fibre of your soul
By overcoming them you'll find you've won
   The blessings of the Lord; your goal.

It's worth every effort you can spend
　In making sure your best you've done
For happiness can have no end
　In the Celestial Kingdom of God and Son.
May Heaven's blessings guide you through
　We pray for you each day.
And may His guiding light guard you
　And keep you safe for us always.

ONE MISSION AND ON AND ANOTHER

A long time elapsed it seemed to us here
Before Michael Wettstein finally returned
From his mission so far from his family so dear
And his friends for his presence all yearned.

Well, Michael returned and apparently needed
More than Scriptures and home ties and all former
    scenes
Though these were important, someone finally
    succeeded
In learning the facts of his well guarded schemes.

The next thing we knew, the secret came out
And this kept the hot lines all humming -
For all were excited and talking about
The girl friend of Michael's who was coming.

Michael's parents received her as an honored guest
In their home for the time the young couple desired
For this Michael and Faizilee planned at their request
To become better acquainted in the time they
    required.

Soon, even a blind man could tell at a glance
Michael had found the girl of whom he had dreamed
And Faizilee seemed equally filled with romance
As the sparks of love kindled and radiantly beamed.

What did they discuss as they walked hand in hand
In this beautiful land of tall trees?
As they were at liberty in Canada land
To discuss all their feelings with ease.

One advantage they had they could freely choose
Any subject that came to their mind
For French was the language they'd conveniently use
No eaves-dropping siblings lurked ever behind.

The engagement announcement was no big surprise
And in the temple of God so secure
In the town of Cardston, Alberta, was solemnized
Their marriage by authority made sure.

And we with this couple testify too
In the faith that forever they're wed
Not just for the duration of life do we view
That marriage is ended as soon as we're dead.

Now lets turn the clock back to where these
      sweethearts met
And review the events to this date
What brought them together; how was the stage set
Or was it a cute trick of fate?

Such a spiritual meeting wasn't begun here on earth
But pre-existed in heaven above
And came with faint whisperings and a rebirth
In their mortal existence with love.

Is it a coincidence that Michael was sent
On a mission to that far distant land
At this very time? It was not his intent
To seek out his future wife's hand.

Does it seem strange to you that Faizilee came
From her homeland of Algeria
And travel to France at the proper time
To charm the blonde prince she was unaware of?

Believe as you wish: the choice is for you
To accept or reject as you please
But to better acquaint you with the couple just view
The events of their romance are these.

In an L.D.S. home of a member in France
Michael and Faizilee met.
And as opposites attract as in this circumstance
A handsome young blonde and a lovely brunette.

But they were alike in other ways that appeal
Where spirituality and intelligence abound
Their sensitive natures knew the Father reveal
Their desire to serve Him is profound.

Both were reserved and could live honorably
Determined by both a good example to set,
These feelings were sensed though discreet they must
    be
For Michael's release was not given him yet.

What a lot of goals and dreams to fulfill
With Michael pursuing perfection
In a righteous home with Faizilee and children
Cooking, poetry, writing, crocheting, sewing and
    then;

Decorating, painting, reading, and love
For family ties and a wonderful living
For sweet memories of loved ones
It all sheds the light on the fact so revealing
That such an ambitious pair having done
Even half of these things would have no time for
    quarreling.

But just in the case there exists one little flaw
That might enter even families best regulated
In marriage it's safe to consider each law
To ensure that your love-life won't be inundated:

1. Never both be angry at the same time I desire.

2. Never yell at each other unless the house is on
fire.

3. Yield to the other's wishes in self discipline. Experience proves it's the best way to win.

4. If you have a choice between making yourself or your mate look good in other's view, choose your mate - you'll look good if you do.

5. If you feel you must criticize do so lovingly.

6. Never bring up a mistake of the past it only makes you feel more ugly.

7. Neglect the whole world rather than each other.

8. Never let the day end without saying at least one complimentary thing to your eternal life's partner.

9. Never meet without an affectionate welcome or embrace.

10. Never go to bed mad. Become reconciled; your troubles erase.

11. When you've made a mistake, talk it out so forgiveness can proceed. An unforgiving partner is most miserable indeed.

12. Remember it takes two to make an argument. The one who is wrong is the one who talks long.

Ogden Nash says it this way:

> *"To keep your marriage brimming*
> *With love in the loving cup*
> *Whenever you're wrong admit it*
> *When you're right, shut up."*

And before I shut up may I say
"May you Michael and Faizilee
Live forever together
In a wonderful world of love
Filled with cherished memories
In the years that are never quite long enough
To hold all your tears and joys."

TO CHRIS WETTSTEIN

(July 10, 1980)

With fondness we recall that day
When you were just a lad
You gave a precious gift away
A billfold you had made by hand

It was at Christmas time as we recall
We two old folk were homesick and blue
You'd chosen Milo for this gift;
It was so very kind of you.

Your family took us home with them
To warmth and joy and glee,
With food galore to share with us;
What jovial company!

We've always been so well impressed
With the radiance of your smile
And personality you possess
Give boosts to our morale.

Your songs and plays and skits in Church
You acted out with Brother
Still bring a chuckle to our minds
As we reminisce together.

Then when I came to babysit
And you would help with cooking
Just proves you'll make a go of it
All this! And so darn good-looking!

So beautifully you dance I note
With lassies quite petite,
It makes a lump come to my throat
Oh that I could my youth repeat!

This wasn't meant for silly rhyme
Sincere is every word
You are so precious to us all
Please don't think this absurd.

Of course to this we must confess
You can be exasperating
If we should say you're perfect Chris
We'd be exaggerating.

But we have world's of faith in you
You're made of "real good stuff."
You'll develop your self discipline
To help guide you when things get tough.

Self discipline is more than self control.
It's value you must rate
In propelling you to win your goal,
Don't underestimate.

Be true to those who trust you, Chris,
True friends enrich your life. And so
Remember all your friends at home
And family prayers go where you go.

Be mindful you're the Father's son
Don't underrate your worth,
It's true that you're the only one
God made like you on earth.

He foreordained you for this time
And special place for you to fill.
Entrusted you with priesthood so divine
To do with as you will.

The Lord has blessed you and he hopes
Your call you'll magnify. And be
As great as in premortal life
And blessed through all eternity.

Entertain upbuilding thoughts
"Hitch your wagon to a star"
What you think about when you don't have to think
Proves what you really are.

Do things that are hard to do
Do your best each precious hour
The next hour will be easier for you
With help in wisdom from God's power.

Give heed to His inspiration; pray
And ask for courage and kind heart;
If you encounter vice or discouragement some day
Command that Satan must depart.

Hold high your head and in your heart rejoice
Though in humility; have faith
And happiness will be your day
If you will heed the Master's voice
And walk the narrow way.

We're glad you came to Rimbey Branch this while.
We hope when you depart
Though tears may splash upon a smile
You'll remember you're still in each one's heart.

MARRIAGE VIEWS and VOWS
(August 15, 1981)

Cheryl and John are unique in the fact,
As most of us came to discover
While they searched records of the past
Behold! They discovered each other!

They found nothing so exciting in records at first
In their efforts in relationships traced
But progress developed as new interests burst;
Their quest for the dead was slightly displaced.

The telephone wires became overworked
As well as the postoffice crew
Causing workers to strike and duties to shirk,
While John's and Cheryl's romance yet grew.

We had thought Cheryl's objectives were seriously
       bent
Upon getting a Master's Degree
In the teaching profession; great efforts were spent
As she obtained a plus efficiency.

Then suddenly as if out of the blue
A bolt of enlightenment struck,
Replacing the M.A. Degree from her view
For an MRS. - we deduct.

Our Cheryl is master of talents galore,
And her teaching will become more renowned
In her home or in Church, we can be sure
This happy musician will surely be found.

Ours was the Branch of the Church where she grew
To learn of the Gospel; where she was baptized
Where she gained a testimony the Gospel is true,
And served in her callings with pride.

Ours is the Branch of the Church where now
She pledges to John her true love
To be solemnized later in the Temple, and vow
To be united on earth and in heaven above.

May you always be happy and have much success
In the joy of achieving together.
Let every quarrel end in a caress,
So that nothing your love-life will sever.

Don't let the sun set on a harbored distress
Nor confer every problem to Mother.
When you're wrong admit it's just selfishness
When you're right - keep still - sister or brother.

Remember to say "I love you", keep holding hands
Even at age ninety-eight.
Let your circle of love include love of both lands,
Commune with your loved ones who anxiously wait.

Don't take love for granted and go your own way
Thinking all will continue the same.
If you fail to add fuel to your courtship each day
You may find you've extinguished the flame.

Petty faults you can find if you're looking for them,
Angel wings droop and halos will tarnish.
You'll find after all you're both human - but then
That's no reason to let your love vanish.

Happiness isn't demanding perfection from each
Though throughout all your life you pursue it.
Cultivate patience, flexibility, understanding, beseech
Not the bride to eat liver soup just to prove it.

Happiness is the capacity to forgive and forget
And developing a good sense of humor.
Have faith in each other; never daring to let
Anyone shake it with some silly rumor.

Create an atmosphere in which each other can grow
And find room for the things of the Spirit.
Search for the good and goodness you know
Will reside when you strive to dwell near it.

Happiness isn't marrying the right one alone
But in being the right partner too.
Live righteously and happiness will abide in your
        home
For the Spirit of God will then dwell with you.

"Our best to you, May your dreams come true,
May old Father Time never be unkind..."

    (This poem was written for Cheryl Langmuir and John Longmuir).

BLESS THIS HOME

Bless this home Oh Lord we pray
With thy love both night and day.
    Bless loved ones who dwell herein
From their toes up past their chin.
    Bless Michael so straight and tall
Bless Shawn, Devin, Trent, Kendall.
    Bless Lenore so kind and good
Training offspring to manhood.
    Bless the kitchen from whose call
"Come and get it," pleases all.
    Blessing the dining room where they
Gather all the family.
    Bowing heads in reverent mood
To thank thee for their home and food.
    Bless the windows and the walls
Framing beauty, sheltered calls.
    Of friends who came to ring their bell
And welcomed in to wish them well.
    Bless all this house Oh Lord we pray
Protect from evil night and day.
    Their home and thine so sacred be
Contained with full felicity.
    Wherein thy spirit sweet abides
Within each soul discerned resides.
    Bless each effort they have spent
In serving thee, with sweet content.

And may they know our prayer shall be
Please bless this home eternally.

*This poem was written for a "house warming" for the
Cahoons after they had moved out of their trailer house and into
the new house they built.*

FAREWELL DEAR FRIENDS
(March 25, 1983)

It seems that time just won't stand still
As we are wont to have it so
When friends like Coads seem bound they will
Fly to the north land; They must go
And "make a mint", and we feel glad
They're being blessed with much success
But on the other hand, we're sad
And mixed emotions fill our breasts,
We have to laugh when we recall
The wit of Randy, and his pranks;
But shed a tear when curtains fall
On such a brief time but our "Thanks"
For sharing with us one brief glance
Of fun and laughter for a while.
Your lovely family is such a joy
With Brenda mothering her brood.
Each sweet freckled girl and boy
Made us all happy. They're so good;
We'll grant they're full of mischief too
A very normal flock.
Randy, they pattern after you
Like "Chips off the old block,"
There are Paul and Lisa and Arlene dear
With Ryan and Melissa nearby
And again within two years
We hear another baby cry.

It's little Adam Phillip who has come
To even up the team-
  Of three and three, a cozy sum
By an old fashioned whim.
  However this computer age
Dotes on the number ten.
  Now can we count you will engage
In continuing in this multiple trend?
  So many children come to earth
Who act like a demon's cousin,
  But yours you train from early birth
We wish you'd have at least a dozen,
  When you your fortune have obtained
And have climbed the topmost rung
  Of success; please come back again
And teach us all how it is done.
  But rich or poor remember us
As onward on this earth's sojourn
  You travel; Our love and trust
Are yours 'til you return
  Or venture to some other places.
We wish you well where e'er you go
  Some others will enjoy your smiling faces,
And love you just as we do.
  We'll think of you and thank you for
The many services you've rendered
  In helping Rimbey Branch run smoother
In Sunday School and Boy Scouts

And the compassionate services you've tendered
In Relief Society, Primary, or other
   Offices or positions with sweet accord
You cheerfully and devotedly filled
   Making us glad, and pleasing the Lord.
We hope to grow to emulate
   Your good example and to live
To be patient, tolerant, and relate
   To wisdom as you've been able to give.
So many words we could multiply
   In praising Coads, revealing facts
By adding all the assets we'd supply
   Another sheet for income tax.
But now our losses give us pain
   As we subtract this family.
Our loss is someone else's gain
   That leaves us feeling Oh! So empty!
Au revoir, and God's speed
   To you and all your clan.
May you be blessed in your every need
   And please return when e'er you can
We've been so richly blessed by you
   We're truly in your debt
But trust all contacts (contracts) you'll renew
   And cancel dues you can't collect.
Fare thee well! Dear friends "Adieu"
   Fond memories we'll ever hold,
Of you, and pray you too

Will never let your love grow cold.
Whatever else may frigid be
  So near to the North Star
May you remain eternally
  Our dear warm friends as you now are.

IRISH SMILES OF BRENDA COAD

Dear Brenda you are leaving
With your family, North to stay
We can hardly keep from grieving
But we knows it's best this way.

Sure Brenda you'll keep smiling
Whether sorrow or in pain
For you know that on the morrow
Sunshine always follows rain.

Your sweet ways are beguiling
They swept Randy off his feet
Sure there's no use in denying
No Colleen is half so sweet.

We're glad you left your home land
Where the four leaf shamrocks grow
In the green lands of dear Ireland
You're the sweetest Irish rose.

You came and found your true love
In a land you found as fair
And the prince you found here waiting
Will your joy forever share.

Dear Brenda keep on smiling
And as sure as you were born
All life's roses you're revising
With a minimum of thorns.

You'll make your whole life happy
And your troubles reconcile
We will treasure a fond memory
Of the sunshine of your smile.

HAPPY LANDING RENNAKERS!

Some people plant their roots so deep
They do not wish to go away.
   Then there are some who seem to keep
Moving around; they will not stay.
   But they can manage very well
And this clever trick achieve
   For each will cast a unique spell;
They'll steal your heart before they leave.

This Branch recalls their efforts made
In missionary work o'er ice and snow
   Seeking the sheep the Master bade
Them feed and help their spirits grow.
   But little ones were left at home
Awaiting parents' late return
   They didn't like to be alone
But patience they must early learn.

Decisions count on many true, brave
men, rendering Gods' word
   He asks to seek out souls to save
But never families shirk.
   Considering the Master's word
And little childrens' pleas
   The family counseled with the Lord
Through fasting and on bended knees.

Durell determined he would please
The Master more by staying home
Helping Marie her burdens ease
While waiting for her unborn son.
Then later on when time was right
Her new arrival came
On March 19th by Angel flight;
Thomas Perry was his name.

Now Church assignments drew a short breath
Which is the Mormon rule.
We see Durell half scared to death
Presiding over Sunday School.
Marie taught well in Primary,
Relief Society, and Seminary too.
She studied genealogy
Just as we all should do.
In Primary, Sunday School, and Sacrament
Marie lead singing on
Her sweet voice rich in fine talent
Inspiring all to join in song.
The youngsters all are learning fast
In Rimbey Branch each week
Lisa and Tracy have advanced
To teachers of Pre-Primary.

Chad Irvin is a deacon now
And serving faithfully
He is a good example of how
To worship reverently.
Kathy and Jason have been baptized
And Thomas thinks he's next
He thinks he's just as old and wise
These grown-up minds have him perplexed.

Oretta is so grown up too
This fall she goes to school
Entering a world to her so new
Exciting, yet she thinks "real cool."
Now Darren you will tutor "Tom"
And teach him all that's good.
You take the lead; he'll follow you,
Don't let him travel the wrong road.

You'll miss Oretta when school's on
But you'll have work to do
In helping Mother care for Tom
And helping Daddy too.
Please don't forget the fun we've had
I'm sure we never will.
The songs you sang and jokes from Dad and Chad
While enjoying Mother's meals.

Your mother has the sweetest smile
With love and understanding too
    She's never selfish but all the while
Her one concern is you.
    Be happy on your newest ranch
Know this; you'll always find
    You're welcome back in Rimbey Branch
In case you change your mind.

HAPPY ANNIVERSARY TO WALTER AND MARGARET

(December 27, 1986)

Margaret and Walter, we're so proud of you
For keeping your vows you made long ago.
You pledged to each other you'd always be true
Come sunshine or sorrow, come rain or come snow.

Your love has sustained you through these forty
      years,
Though they didn't flow softly like a summer breeze
No one ever promised there wouldn't be tears
Nor a life filled with roses and ease.

You have weathered the test and proved without
      doubt
Those storm clouds were never for real,
Though rumbling and roaring occasionally came out
They just brought you closer - your love to reveal.

And by airing your problems you could best
      understand
As you sobbed on each other's shoulder,
You'd wipe away tears and hold each other's hand
Secure in more wisdom and mature as you're older.

You worked on your farm with Rimbey near by
Earning your living by the sweat of your brows,
Margaret a housewife; making bread or a pie
Pleasing Walter who worked in the field and with
      cows.

But best of all crops that you ever had
Were favored and nurtured successfully
Promoted you to status of proud Mother and Dad
When you reared your own lovely family tree.

There were Darlene and Gayla and Sheila and Cheryl
Four little angels at work or at play.
A million dollars couldn't buy one little girl
But when they grew up Walter gave them away.

He wouldn't admit any wrong he had done
Though mixed feelings he felt at the altar
He rationalized feebly he was gaining a son
And not really losing a daughter.

Time proved he was right and quite naturally
As days drifted by and the years rolled around
New little twigs appeared on his family tree
And more joyful grandparents can never be found.

Abundance of joy resides in their home
As each one is welcomed therein.
Two beautiful nieces deemed them as their own
Loving parents; dear Nancy and Lynn.

Margaret and Walter you became "citified"
As you moved into Rimbey from farm and hard toil
In your spacious newest home you're more satisfied
Since time permits you those grandchildren to spoil.

So many ambitions you always possessed
In remembering and recounting they're hard to recall
The most noteworthy one with which you've been
      blessed
Are your spiritual achievements most important of
      all.

Praises to you for the goals you have set
Pray that no evil influence or impulsive endeavor
Thwart your lofty ideals and cause you to forget
The promise that "Families can be forever."

Fight to the end "ruby anniversary" friends;
I'm proud you're my sister and brother,
But may I make clear that "fight to the end"
Means endure; Let's not fight with each other.

Just keep up the fight in doing what's right
Many years you have yet for your harvest
You're far in arrears in reaching your "golden years"
Buckle up! The first hundred years are the hardest!

(This poem was sent to Cheryl and John Longmuir in Edmonton, Alberta, Canada, in answer to their request and invitation to attend the fortieth anniversary of Cheryl's parents, Walter and Margaret Langmuir. The copy was sent by registered mail on November 29, 1986).

MILO'S AND LILLIAN'S FIFTIETH ANNIVERSARY

A cowboy met a teacher on a Wyoming ranch
On a roundup of the future in the ensuing romance.
The time wasn't wasted; soon after they met
Wedding plans were made and a certain date set.

Their vows were exchanged; they of course didn't
   know
What challenges they'd face as together they'd go
Through advancing years of joy and despair
Some changes were made; Milo learned to cut hair.

Lillian fondly remembers school days that are gone
Still rejoicing in good work her students have done.
Now the family is planning for "Mike" and his
   spouse
A brief get-together in the L.D.S. Meeting House.

In Worland, Wyoming, June 4, 1988
From 2 until 4 P.M. They can't stay up late.
They can't think of anything more joyful to do
Than to have the privilege of chatting with you.

In honor of fifty years of their married life
Of one Milo Leithead and Lillian his wife.
Lillian insists married life isn't bad.
It's the best fifty years that they've ever had.

(This is the invitation that the author wrote for their 50th wedding anniversary).

GRATITUDE

"It is easy enough to be happy
When life flows along like a song
But the one worthwhile, is the one who can smile
When everything goes dead wrong."

These lines were borrowed from someone
With a lesson worth keeping in mind,
In our challenge in everyday living
For success in much happiness find.

Each breath I take on this planet
Is a gift of such infinite worth
Bestowed by the Heavenly Father
In enhancing my spirit by birth.

I'm blessed by having the wisdom
In accepting the plan of the Lord,
And born in this last dispensation
With free agency; an added award.

I'm grateful to be of some service
However small that may be,
May I sometime set forth an example
Of honest and true charity.

I hope to attain exaltation
Though I have such a long way to go,
My friends are a great inspiration
So willing to teach and to show

Their love and their patience forever
Expressed in kind words and they share
Experiences that are uplifting
That strengthen and solace me here.

My best friend, of course, is my husband.
He is helpful, he is faithful, he is kind
Our marriage is sealed in the temple
By the priesthood ordained, so divine.

Again, may I say I am grateful
For each trial and blessing of love,
And gifts given me to develop
Bestowed from the Heaven above.

THOSE GOLDEN YEARS

Guests were most welcome in the Dunning Cafe
In the years we are pleased to recall.
Fifty years have gone by and we shall now try
To review some events, but not all.

Cowboys were swelling the ranks of the town
During days of the Blaine County Fair.
Leon was among them - a classy young man
With sparkling blue eyes and dark curly hair.

He strode down the street toward the cafe
To buy some good food and to meet
A waitress whom he might persuade
To go out with him on a date.

The waitress he found was appealing to him
As she came to his table to serve.
He tried hard to think of a yarn he could spin
While bolstering up all his nerve.

He thought a slight joke might impress her the most;
He ignored the usual entree.
When he soberly ordered a whale on some toast
Clara thought he was "out of his tree."

Well Clara was good looking and Leon liked her
        cooking
You guessed it; they started to date.
Before very long he was crooning this song
We'll have to admit it's first rate.

"Please don't serve coffee and apple pie
To anyone else but me
My honey girl don't you see,
I crave your company."

"Just say 'I do,'
And I'll prove to you
How happy we can be
- On my father's farm."

Thedford's Judge tied the knot
But Clara forgot
To tell her mother her plan.
Fireworks flew
As newspapers were viewed

And revealed the "sly trick"
Of that man —
Who stole her young daughter
To alter her brand.

Clara's mother had taught her, her dear little daughter
To avoid all the men and their strife,
"Married life was a slaughter, and she had just
        oughter
Stay single the rest of her life."

Before very long Leon altered his song
As most fun seemed darkly discarded;
"Well I didn't mean the grass would always be green
I never promised you a rose garden."

Times seemed very bleak as they left Brewster to
        seek
A way to find better employ.
They went to the West to build a new nest
And took with them their first baby boy.

The dairy in Rawlins, Wyoming, was first
To consider their needs for good pay
But the work was so hard and not worth the reward
While slaving their young lives away.

Saratoga, Wyoming, offered employment too
On a ranch that looked better to them.
They gained a few dollars and another wee son
And returned to Nebraska again.

The babies won hearts as most grandchildren can;
Carl and Roy weren't any exception.
Heaven and earth were now in command;
These darlings got a royal reception.

Arrangements were made with the children in mind
To obtain a permanent home.
Southwest of Merna, Nebraska, we find
This family has multiplied some.

There were Carl, Roy, Iris, Janice, and Gerald
Then Georgia, Kathleen, and Roger (the last son)
Because Clara decided this crop had increased
Enough for their needs; she was done.

The mixed farming and ranching have served them
        quite well
But not without hardships in growing;
The family can all very expertly tell
"When the going gets tough - the tough just get
        going."

The kids went to school in Merna, of course,
Which captured their parents' attention.
Music and ball games - the greatest resort;
Academics - the dullest invention.

History repeats itself as we can observe,
The kids all grew up and found spouses,
And they in their turn have their own little herd
In each one's own separate houses.

Now Clara and Leon, retired, can proudly boast
Of children, grandchildren, and greats.
Leon is now trying to catch the whale for the toast
As he fishes on oceans and lakes.

We congratulate both of you for keeping your vows
You made in those fifty years past.
We love you and pray that God will allow
Many more years of the best.

(Lovingly written for the year 1989 honoring Clara and Leon Hunt on their fiftieth wedding anniversary. Clara is the author's sister).

GUS AND FRANCES WHIPPLE'S 60th
ANNIVERSARY

In Long Beach, California at a Valentine's dance
A beautiful couple formed a budding romance,
As each other's charms they soon were aware,
Embraced in a honeymoon forever to share.

Gus Whipple and Frances Willis met in that way
And became husband and wife on the 25th of May.
They traveled life's highways of joys and some tears
So true to each other these sixty-five (65) years.

In the Mesa Arizona temple their marriage was
    sealed
By divine authority; the Lord has revealed:
Families can be forever through covenants kept
When ordinances of Priesthood in true spirit accept.

May your love and devotion always remain
As you walk hand in hand down True Lovers' Lane.
Endure to the end of your sojourn on earth
Fulfilling the purpose of your mortal birth.

To the descendants of Gus and Frances so dear
You have a noble heritage given you here.
Cherish and follow the examples they've set
Rewarding their love for which you're in debt

Until you become the best you can be
Attaining the realms of the highest degree.
Many are blessed as their lives have been touched
By Frances and Gus whom are loved very much.

TO BILLY BARNES

Good-night Darling, there'll be a great round-up
When we too have advanced thru' the veil
Where no sorrows or sadness are found up
Along that glorious trail.

We'll behold your heavenly greeting
And again sense your loving embrace
Rejoicing in sacred reunion
Eternal - in God's holy place.

On earth you shared God's Holy Priesthood
And taught the Gospel to men
So by living the laws God has given
We are happily united again.

Our pattern of life interrupted
Temporily only - we know
To prove ourselves worthy and trusted
To follow His plan here below.

So good-night; we will work for the round-up
And cherish your memories still
There'll be no mavericks among us
When we meet at the top of the hill.

ALVENA'S RETURN HOME
Mrs Billy (Alvena) Barnes

My darling, I've joined the great round-up
I too, have advanced through the veil.
Our suffering and sorrows have ended
As we meet on this Heavenward Trail.

I behold your radiant greeting
And rejoice in your loving embrace
As we partake of the blessings of Priesthood
The eternal gift of God's grace.

He has prepared us a home in His Heaven;
How peaceful Our Father's Abode!
Our place with the blessed He has given
And release from the Earth's weary load.

We look to loved ones left behind us
With loving and tender concern;
Praying you will be watchful and faithful
'Til the day of the Saviour's return.

Live the laws of God in the Gospel
That the Father has given to man
So we may have a reunion
With our families in heaven again.

Goodnight loves, we'll see you tomorrow
In Earth's Round-up and be it God's will
You too shall be released from all sorrow:
And we'll meet at the top of the hill.

GOD'S "GOING AWAY" PLANNED

Some flowers bloom all through the summer
Some flowers bloom just for a day,
And somehow there must be a reason
They are suddenly taken away.

Each creature that ever inhabits
This planet; our glorious earth
Was created by Heavenly Father
And sent on a mission through birth.

We wanted to grow to be like Him,
Rejoiced in His wisdom and plan
E'en though there'd be pain and much sorrow
Inflicted upon every man.

Don't despair if the load seems too heavy
Let your faith and your prayers all employ
The blessing the Father has promised:
"Men are that they may have joy."

Surely Rodney has fulfilled his mission
On earth, he was sent forth to do,
And is now with his Heavenly Father
Waiting, praying, for me and for you.

(A farewell to Rodney Fowler)

FAREWELL TO FELMA
(Felma Fowler)

Good-night Felma, we'll see you tomorrow
When we too have advanced through the veil
And progressed through this valley of sorrow
To leave all our earthly travail.

We'll rejoice in our family reunion
When you meet us and give us your hand
To welcome in holy communion
With the Heavenly Father you've planned.

We'll know by your warm friendly greeting
And the radiant smile on your face
You've faithfully worked for this meeting
At your table there's always a place.

As even on earth you were gracious
Your relationships were without flaw
To the girls in your family you were "Mother"
And not just a mother-in-law.

You were generous in sharing the Gospel
You were eager to help everyone
And happy in reading the scriptures
To Jeana, each week you with sisters would come.

Oh, how your heart sang when you opened
The letters you got in the mail
From your son whom you sent on a mission
To Scotland, so blessed was Dale.

The other boys too were a blessing
Along with their good-natured dad
And precious grandchildren caressing
Such loving grandparents they had.

We're thankful for memories you left us
And the pictures you gave by the score
To all of your friends as you blessed us
With these treasures we'll keep evermore.

Your testimony of the true living Gospel
Was your greatest blessing by far
And each life you touched became richer
And helped us become what we are.

Now we will remember your teachings,
We'll try to live up to them all
'Til the Master will hear our beseechings
And, we'll meet you again through the veil.

TO EMERON, WITH LOVE

As I look out on the meadows green
And across to the mountains in their lofty air
With the birds singing sweetly; the earth so serene,
Except for a loneliness because you're not there.

Then whispers float softly from your heavenly sphere
To me in my earthly abode,
Sending pity to me because I'm still here
While you are relieved from your burdensome load.

Your school of hard knocks is now in the past,
With your many achievements well done.
You too are a graduate from life's worldly tests,
Mortality's challenge accepted and won.

The knowledge you've gained is remaining with you;
Your gold and your silver are gone.
Eternal progression is your's to add to;
Your talents develop in your heavenly home.

"As ye have done it unto the least of these"
Was our Savior's fond admonition.
We all rest assured that He is well pleased
With your natural Godward rendition.

To all of your neighbors and friends you were pure
In unselfish acts without any guile.
Your dealings with fellow men trustworthy and sure
With honesty given with love and a smile.

"Blessed are the peacemakers," applies also to you
Instilled in your heart when you were yet young
Avoiding most troubles you very well knew
It was wisdom in keeping a well-bridled tongue.

"Tall in the saddle", you surely did ride
From the dawn to the setting of sun.
You took responsibilities well in your stride
And worked until tasks were skillfully done.

Your family was ever your pride and your joy
Your wife, your son, and your daughter.
The in-laws too were all very choice
As the kids eventually advanced to the altar.

No other grand kids were one-half as neat
As those of Emeron and Mary.
The grandstand contained their two reserved seats;
It seemed that some games were quite scary.

In life our roundups will come and they go,
And games we too maybe sever,
But the greatest roundup that we'll ever know
Is when our families all gather together, forever.

DEAR MARY

Dear Mary, the Lord has released you,
From confusion, suffering, and pain
To progress through the veil to your loved ones
Who were waiting to join you again,

Your Aunt and your Uncle who reared you
As a substitute Mother and Dad
Considered your former bereavements
And gave you the best that they had.

You treasured their love with all others
Who were fortunate to visit your home.
Your fun-loving sister and brothers
All knew they were welcome to come.

You've weathered life's tempests and hardships;
Hard work was no stranger to you,
Each duty was done with full measure,
With a knack and a knowledge of just what to do.

Your talents in modern day living
By many are now overlooked.
No computer could ever be programmed
To plan or excel banquet meals like you cooked.

Mary didn't know how to be selfish;
Her concern was for others' welfare.
You couldn't be hungry or lonely,
So soon were you under her care.

She was usually meek and submissive;
But was ready to stand up and fight
If she judged a loved one was mistreated
She insisted that all wrongs were made right.

Her husband and children were blessings;
Her grandchildren a source of great joy.
It is hard to find words in expressing
The depth of the love she employed.

Our lives have all been made richer
In knowing this dear one and friend.
We take comfort in knowing this sister
Has fought a good fight to the end.

She has won her reward with the Father,
And we too can eventually share
If we will strive to live worthy
Her joy in rejoining her there.

(This poem was written in tribute to Mary Leithead, Emeron Leithead's wife).

TO LEOMA

Dear Leoma, we'll all sorely miss you,
Your compassion and love so divine;
The Lord in His wisdom has blessed you
In your submission of "Not my will, but thine".

Your patience and kind understanding,
Your jovial good nature shone through;
You were a true friend and companion
To your dear ones and all who knew you.

We would all profit much if we'd follow
Your example in perfection maintained
Every task you skillfully rendered
No unfinished duty remained.

And now that your labors are over
On earth, and your mission nobly done;
We take comfort in the exquisite joy that awaits you
Beyond the veil with your other loved ones.

Our parting is but a small moment
Compared with eternity fair,
There'll be a marvelous family reunion
With our loved ones eternally there.

This promise was made by Heavenly Father
In good faith we can always be sure
If we will serve Him and each other
And to the end of our short time endure.

(Written as a tribute to Leoma, Darwin Leithead's wife).

THE MONTHS

January, full of cheer
Ushers in a brand new year.

February brings to minds
Presidents and valentines.

March brings patterns very bright
Glowing on each flying kite.

April still brings breezes cool
Boys play marbles near the school.

May brings warmth and springtime showers
Waking up the pretty flowers.

June is time for school vacation
Summer camps and recreation.

Hot July brings rodeos,
Fishing trips and outdoor shows.

August hails the gay bazaars;
Carnivals with kiddie cars.

Gay September still is warm.
Back to school the children swarm.

When October's frost is keen
We'll watch out for Hallowe'en.

In November we keep living
For the day that means Thanksgiving.

Gay December full of mirth
Marks the blessed Savior's birth.

GREETINGS FROM WYOMING

A big "Howdy" from Worland, Wyoming
And my "Thanks" for warm friendship and fun
Hospitality from Arizona
Can hardly be matched or outdone.

But if you would come to Wyoming
We'd love to just give it a try
In the shade of our cool lofty mountains
That seem to shake hands with the sky.

We love our great wide-open spaces
Where the deer and the antelope roam
We have generous smiles on our faces
In our pride for the place we call home.

"Womens lib" is "old hat" in Wyoming
Where equality and suffrage began
Where our Nation's first National Monument
And Yellowstone Park are so grand.

Girl Scouts Center West in our mountains
And the Tyrolean Band in our town
Inspire and give hope to the critics
Much good in our youth can be found.

Our sugar beets sweeten your beverage
And our lamb chops and pork chops are fine
There are dairies and beef to your liking
And steaks that are superbly prime.

Now before you deem this a commercial
And are tempted to just tune me out
This message: Come visit Wyoming
And you'll see what I'm talking about.

(Written for a friend who was a delegate to a DOE'S Convention in Arizona).

LINDA AND BILL

Dear Linda and Bill, know we love you
And remind you in our humble way
You have left home and angels above you
Are taking note of how you obey
The vows that you made in the heavens
Nobly keeping well your First Estate.
Don't "blow it" and join with old Satan;
Dismiss him before it's too late.

Of course you may find it "tough sledding"
To go the way you know is best
So "gird up your loins" and start treading
The straight way to God; it's your test.
God will assist you after you've "shown your stuff"
Nothing easy was ever worthwhile
Happiness comes if you work hard enough
Blessings come after tribulation and trial.

God won't do for you what you can do for yourself.
He's given you all that you need.
With Scriptures and Prophets and Patriarch's help
And free agency to ignore or to heed.
Will you accept Him; Be tried and be true
Fight to finish what you've started on earth
To succeed or to fail; it's all up to you
At the end of life's journey, what will you be worth?

"Mom"